You Must Be Joking!!!
Second Edition

*A collection of
jokes, quotes & stories
from the internet.*

Collected & Compiled by
Tim & Rick Stapenhurst

Stapenhurst
SP
Publications

The editors have made every reasonable effort to identify and contact potential copyright holders. We have also checked attributions and have made acknowledgements where possible. Where we have not made attributions we have not been able to identify or confirm them. Any errors that may have occurred are inadvertent and anyone who for any reason has not been contacted is invited to write to the editors so that full acknowledgement may be made in subsequent editions of the book. We welcome information regarding non-attributed material and will use such information to adjust attributions in the future.

info@stapenhurstpublications.com

First Edition: 2015
Second Edition: 2017

ISBN-13:9781979821018

ACKNOWLEDGEMENT & DEDICATION

We admire and would like to thank those who developed the material in this book. We wish we were as clever as they are! Without you we wouldn't laugh so much, there would be no book and the charities would not benefit from the proceeds.

We also thank those who emailed us the jokes: David Beare (who wins the prize for sending us the most), Aideen McCrave, Mary McQuillan, Andrew Hall, Joan Fowler, Irene Wilson, Steve Stuart, John Killman, Carola Schwabl, Jack Titsworth and Sandra Ecrit. You brought a lot of laughter into our lives over the years when you sent these jokes, and we laughed just as much as we collated this book.

We thank the charities that will benefit from the proceeds of sales of this book: churches, orphanages, schools and overseas aid organisations. You do so much good work and touch so many lives. We hope that the proceeds from the sale of this book will help you to continue the work you do.

Finally, we thank those of you who are supporting the charities by buying this book. We hope you enjoy it as much as we enjoyed collating it.

CONTENTS

1 Laugh 'Till You Cry

Inner Strength

If you can start the day without caffeine or pep pills,

If you can be cheerful, ignoring aches and pains,

If you can resist complaining and boring people with your troubles,

If you can eat the same food everyday and be grateful for it,

If you can understand when loved ones are too busy to give you time,

If you can overlook when people take things out on you, through no fault of yours,

If you can take criticism and blame without resentment,

If you can face the world without lies and deceit,

If you can conquer tension without medical help,

If you can relax without liquor,

If you can sleep without the aid of drugs,

If you can do all these things...

Then you are probably the family dog.

☺   ☺   ☺

If people from Poland are called Poles, then why aren't people from Holland called Holes?

Three Men and a River

One day, three men were hiking and unexpectedly came upon a large raging, violent river. They needed to get to the other side, but had no idea of how to do so.

The first man prayed, saying, "Please God, give me the strength to cross this river." Poof! God gave him big arms and strong legs, and he was able to swim across the river in about two hours, after almost drowning a couple of times.

Seeing this, the second man prayed, saying, "Please God, give me the strength... and the tools to cross this river." Poof! God gave him a rowboat and he was able to row across the river in about an hour, after almost capsizing the boat a couple of times.

The third man had seen how this worked out for the other two, so he also prayed saying, "Please God, give me the strength ....and the tools....and the intelligence to cross this river." And poof! God turned him into a woman. She looked at the map, hiked upstream a couple of hundred yards, then walked across the bridge.

Velcro? - What a rip off!

Who Surgeons Prefer to Operate on

Five surgeons are discussing who makes the best patients to operate on. The first surgeon says: "I like to see accountants on my operating table, because when you open them up, everything inside is numbered."

The second responds: "Yeah, but you should try electricians! Everything inside is color coded."

The third surgeon says, "No, I really think librarians are the best; everything inside them is in alphabetical order."

The fourth chimes in: "I like construction workers...those guys always understand when you have a few parts left over at the end and when the job takes longer than you said it would."

But the fifth surgeon shut them all up when he observed: "You're all wrong. Politicians are the easiest to operate on. There's no guts, no heart, and no spine, and the head and backside are interchangeable."

☺   ☺   ☺

A dog gave birth to puppies near the road and was cited for littering.

How to Tame Your Parrot

A young man named John received a parrot as a gift. The problem was the parrot had a bad attitude and an even worse vocabulary. Every word out of the bird's mouth was rude, obnoxious, and laced with profanity. John tried and tried to change the bird's attitude by consistently saying only polite words, playing soft music and anything else he could think of to "clean up" the bird's vocabulary, but to no avail.

Finally, John was fed up and he yelled at the parrot. The parrot yelled back. John shook the parrot and the parrot got angrier and even more rude. In desperation, John threw up his hands, grabbed the bird and put him in the freezer. For a few minutes the parrot squawked and kicked and screamed. Then suddenly, there was total quiet. Not a peep was heard for over a minute.

Fearing that he'd killed the parrot, John quickly opened the door to the freezer. The parrot calmly stepped out onto John's outstretched arm and said, "I believe I may have offended you with my rude language and actions. I am sincerely remorseful for my inappropriate transgressions and I fully intend to do everything I can to correct my rude and unforgivable behaviour."

☞ ☞ ☞

10

John was stunned at the change in the bird's attitude. As he was about to ask the parrot what had made such a dramatic change in his behaviour, the bird continued. "May I ask what the chicken did?"

☺ ☺ ☺

Dumb Tourists

One lovely summer's day two foreign tourists were driving through the Welsh countryside. Arriving at Llanfairpwllgwyngyllgogerychwyrndrobwyllllantysi liogogoch, they stopped for lunch, and one of the tourists asked the waitress: 'Before we order, I wonder if you could settle an argument for us. Will you pronounce where we are, very, very, very slowly?'
The waitress leaned over and said:
"Bur ... ger ... King"

☺ ☺ ☺

The wife was counting all the 5p and 10p coins out on the kitchen table when she suddenly got very angry and started shouting and crying for no reason. I thought to myself, "She's going through the change."

Health Issues? (Don't) Try This...

Do you have feelings of inadequacy?
Do you suffer from shyness?
Do you sometimes wish you were more assertive?

If you answered yes to any of these questions, ask your doctor about Cabernet Sauvignon.

Cabernet Sauvignon is the safe, natural way to feel better and more confident about yourself and your actions. It can help ease you out of your shyness and let you tell the world that you're ready and willing to do just about anything.

You will notice the benefits of Cabernet Sauvignon almost immediately and, with a regimen of regular doses, you can overcome any obstacles that prevent you from living the life to the full.

Shyness and awkwardness will be a thing of the past and you will discover many talents you never knew you had. Stop hiding and start living.

Cabernet Sauvignon may not be right for everyone. Women who are pregnant or nursing should not use it. However, women who wouldn't mind nursing or becoming pregnant are encouraged to try it.

☞ ☞ ☞

Side effects may include:

Dizziness, nausea, vomiting, incarceration, loss of motor control, loss of clothing, loss of money, loss of virginity, delusions of grandeur, table dancing, headache, dehydration, dry mouth, and a desire to sing karaoke and play all-night rounds of strip poker, truth or dare, and naked twister.

Warnings:

The consumption of Cabernet Sauvignon may:

- make you think you are whispering when you are not.
- cause you to tell your friends over and over again that you love them.
- cause you to think you can sing.
- create the illusion that you are tougher, smarter, faster and better looking than most people.

Please feel free to share this important information with as many people as you feel may benefit!

Now just imagine what you could achieve with a good Shiraz or Merlot...

LIFE IS A CABERNET OLD CHUM!

☺   ☺   ☺

If a pig loses its voice, is it disgruntled?

The Bacon Tree

Two Mexicans are lost in the desert. Wandering aimlessly and starving. They are about to just lie down and await death when all of a sudden Luis says.........

"Hey Pepe, do you smell what I smell? Ees bacon, I theenk."

"Ees, Luis, eet sure smell like bacon."

With renewed hope they struggle up the next sand dune, and there, in the distance, is a tree loaded with bacon.

There's raw bacon, there's fried bacon, back bacon, double smoked bacon ... Every imaginable kind of cured pork.

"Pepe, Pepe, wees saved! Ees a bacon tree!"

"Luis, maybe ees a meerage? Wees in the desert don't forget."

"Pepe, since when deed you ever hear of a meerage that smell like bacon...ees no meerage, ees a bacon tree!" And with that, Luis staggers towards the tree.

☞ ☞ ☞

He gets to within 5 metres, Pepe crawling close behind, when suddenly a machine gun opens up, and Luis drops like a wet sock. Mortally wounded, he warns Pepe with his dying breath....

"Pepe... Go back, man, you was right, ees not a bacon tree!"

"Luis, Luis mi amigo... what ees it? "

"Pepe.. ees not a bacon tree. Ees...

Ees...
Ees...
Ees....
Ees...
Ees... a... ham... bush..."

☺   ☺   ☺

Police Officer Quotes

"You know, stop lights don't come any redder than the one you just went through."

"Relax, the handcuffs are tight because they're new. They'll stretch after you wear them a while."

Banned From the Supermarket.

Yesterday I was at my local supermarket buying a large bag of Woofta dog food for my loyal pet. I was in the checkout queue when a woman behind me asked if I had a dog.

What did she think I had: an elephant? So, since I'm retired and have little to do, on impulse I told her that no, I didn't have a dog, I was starting the Woofta Diet again. I added that I probably shouldn't, because I ended up in hospital last time, but I'd lost 30lb (13Kg) before I woke up in intensive care with tubes coming out of most of my orifices and IVs in both arms.

I told her that it was essentially a perfect diet and that the way that it works is to load your pockets with Woofta nuggets and simply eat one or two every time you feel hungry. The food is nutritionally complete so it works well and I was going to try it again. (I have to mention here that practically everyone in the queue was now enthralled with my story.)

Horrified, she asked me if I ended up in intensive care because the dog food poisoned me. I told her no, I ran across the road to chase an Irish Setter and a car hit me.

🐾 🐾 🐾

I thought the guy behind her was going to have a heart attack he was laughing so hard. I'm now banned from shop!

Better watch what you ask retired people. They have all the time in the world to think of daft things to say.

☺ ☺ ☺

How to Replace Expensive Windows.....FREE!

Last year I replaced all the windows in my house with those expensive, double-pane, energy-efficient kind.

Today, I got a call from the contractor who installed them. He complained that the work had been completed a year ago and I still hadn't paid.

Helloooo,... just because I'm blonde doesn't mean that I am stupid. So, I told him just what his fast-talking sales guy told me last year... that these windows would pay for themselves in a year. Helloooo? It's been a year, so they're paid for, I told him. There only silence at the other end of the line, so I finally hung up. He never called back. I bet he felt like an idiot.

The Golf Playing Frog

A man takes the day off work and decides to go out golfing. He is on the second hole when he notices a frog sitting next to the green. He thinks nothing of it and is about to shoot when he hears "Ribbit 9 Iron."

The man looks around and doesn't see anyone.

Again, he hears, "Ribbit 9 iron."

He looks at the frog and decides to prove the frog wrong, puts the club away, and grabs a 9 iron. Boom! He hits the ball 10 inches from the cup. He is shocked.

He says to the frog: "Wow that's amazing! You must be a lucky frog, eh?"

The frog replies: "Ribbit lucky frog."

The man decides to take the frog with him to the next hole. "What do you think frog?" the man asks. "Ribbit 3 wood." comes the reply.

The guy takes out a 3 wood and, Boom! Hole in one... The man is befuddled and doesn't know what to say.

☞ ☞ ☞

By the end of the day, the man golfed the best game of golf in his life and asks the frog: "OK where to next?" The frog replies: 'Ribbit Las Vegas"

They go to Las Vegas and the guy says: "OK frog, now what?" The frog says: "Ribbit Roulette."

Upon approaching the roulette table, the man asks: "What do you think I should bet?" The frog replies: "Ribbit $3000, black 6." Now, this is a million-to-one shot to win, but after the golf game the man figures what the heck.

Boom! Tons of cash comes sliding back across the table. The man takes his winnings and buys the best room in the Hotel.

He sits the frog down and says: "Frog, I don't know how to repay you. You've won me all this money and I am forever grateful." The frog replies: "Ribbit Kiss Me." He figures why not, since after all the frog did for him, he deserves it.

With a kiss, the frog turns into a gorgeous girl.

"And that, your honour, is how the girl ended up in my room. So help me, or my name is not William Jefferson Clinton."

Don't Drink and Drive Your Car: Take a Bus.

I would like to share an experience with you all, about drinking and driving.

As you well know, some of us have been known to have had brushes with the authorities on our way home from the odd social session over the years.

A couple of nights ago, I was out for a few drinks with some friends and had a few too many beers and some rather nice claret. Knowing full well that I may have been slightly over the limit, I did something I've never done before - I took a bus home.

I arrived home safely and without incident, which was a real surprise, as I have never driven a bus before and am not sure where I got it from!

☺   ☺   ☺

I went to the cemetery yesterday to lay some flowers on a grave. As I was standing there I noticed 4 grave diggers walking about with a coffin: 3 hours later and they're still walking about with it. I thought to myself, they've lost the plot!

A Message From Us Golden Oldies

A C-130 military transport aircraft was lumbering along when a cocky F-16 fighter aircraft flashed by. The jet jockey decided to show off.

The fighter jockey called up the C-130 pilot and said: "Watch this!" and promptly went into a barrel roll followed by a steep climb. He then finished with a sonic boom as he broke the sound barrier. The F-16 pilot asked the C-130 pilot: "Waddya think of that!!!"

The C-130 pilot said: "That was impressive, but watch this." The C-130 droned along for about 5 minutes and then the C-130 pilot came back on and asked: "What did you think of that?"

Puzzled, the F-16 pilot asked: "What the heck did you do?" The C-130 pilot chuckled. "I stood up, stretched my legs, walked to the back of the plane, went to the bathroom, then got a cup of coffee and a cinnamon bun."

When you are young & foolish - speed & flash may seem a good thing!!!

When you get older & smarter - comfort & dull is not such a bad thing!!!

 ☺ ☺ ☺

Pulled Over For Doing 22 MPH!

Sitting on the side of the highway waiting to catch speeding drivers, a police officer sees a car puttering along at 22 m.p.h. He says to himself, "This driver is just as dangerous as a speeder!" So he puts on his lights and pulls the driver over.

Approaching the car, he notices there are five old ladies in the vehicle -- two in the front seat and three in the back -- all but the driver are wide-eyed and white as ghosts.

The driver, obviously confused, says to him, "Officer, I don't understand, I was doing exactly the speed limit! What seems to be the problem?" "Ma'am," the officer replies, "you weren't speeding, but you should know that driving slower than the speed limit can also be a danger to other drivers."

"Slower than the speed limit?" says the surprised driver. "No, sir. I was doing the speed limit exactly - 22 miles an hour," the old woman says a bit proudly.

The police officer, trying to contain a chuckle, explains to her that 22 is the highway number, not the speed limit.

☞ ☞ ☞

A bit embarrassed, the woman grins and thanks the officer for pointing out her error.

"Before I let you go, Ma'am," says the officer, "I have to ask: Is everyone in this car OK? These women seem awfully shaken, and they haven't made a peep this whole time," says the officer.

"Oh, they'll be alright in a minute officer," replies the driver. "We just got off Highway 189."

☺　　☺　　☺

Replacing a Fridge

A guy bought a new fridge for his house. To get rid of his old fridge, he put it in his front yard and hung a sign on it saying:
Free to good home. You want it, you take it.

For three days the fridge sat there without anyone looking twice. He eventually decided that people were too mistrustful of this deal. So he changed the sign to read:
Fridge for sale $50.

The next day someone stole it.

☺　　☺　　☺

A backward poet writes inverse.

A Woman Prospector, a Gunslinger and a Mule.

An old woman prospector shuffled into town leading a tired old mule. The old woman headed straight for the only saloon to clear her parched throat.

She walked up and tied her old mule to the hitch rail. As she stood there, brushing some of the dust from her face and clothes, a young gunslinger stepped out of the saloon with a gun in one hand and a bottle of whiskey in the other.

The young gunslinger looked at the old woman and laughed, saying "Hey old woman, have you ever danced?"

The old woman looked up at the gunslinger and said: "No, I never did dance... Never really wanted to."

A crowd had gathered as the gunslinger grinned and said, "Well, you're gonna dance now," and started shooting at the old woman's feet.

The old woman prospector - not wanting to get her toe blown off started hopping around. Everybody was laughing.

☞ ☞ ☞

When his last bullet had been fired, the young gunslinger, still laughing, holstered his gun and turned around to go back into the saloon.

The old woman turned to her pack mule, pulled out a double-barrelled shotgun, and cocked both hammers.

The loud clicks carried clearly through the desert air. The crowd stopped laughing immediately.

The young gunslinger heard the sounds too, and he turned around very slowly. The silence was almost deafening.

The crowd watched as the young gunman stared at the old woman and the large gaping holes of those twin barrels.

The barrels of the shotgun never wavered in the old woman's hands, as she quietly said: "Son, have you ever kissed a mule's backside?"

The gunslinger swallowed hard and said: "No ma'am... but... I've always wanted to."

☞   ☞   ☞

There are a few lessons for us all here:

1 Never be arrogant.
2 Don't waste ammunition.
3 Whiskey makes you think you're smarter than you are.
4 Always, always make sure you know who has the power.
5 Don't mess with old women: they didn't get old by being stupid.

Getting the Car Fixed

A woman takes her car into a garage to have some dents removed. The mechanic knowing she isn't the brightest girl in the world, decides to play a joke on her.

"You don't need me to take those dents out," he says. "Just blow up the exhaust pipe and the metal will pop back into place".

So she takes the car home and tries it.

Her husband spots her from the house, opens a window and shouts "That won't work! You have to wind the windows up first!"

☺   ☺   ☺

Drinking Bet

A Texan walks into a pub renowned for hard drinking and clears his voice to the crowded bar. He says: "I hear you are a bunch of hard drinkers. I'll give 500 American dollars to anybody in here who can drink 10 pints of Guinness back-to-back."

The room is quiet, and no one takes up the Texan's offer. One man even leaves.

Thirty minutes later the same gentleman who left shows up again and taps the Texan on the shoulder. "Is your bet still good?" asks the man.

The Texan says yes and asks the bartender to line up 10 pints of Guinness. Immediately the man tears into all 10 of the pint glasses, drinking them all back-to-back.

The other pub patrons cheer as the Texan stares in amazement. The Texan gives the man the $500 and says, "If ya don't mind me askin', where did you go for that 30 minutes you were gone?"

The man replies, "Oh... I had to go to the pub down the street first, to see if I could do it."

Poor old Ed Loses the Election and Now This

Ed Miliband is (at the time of writing) the leader of the Labour party in the United Kingdom.

Ed Miliband walks into a bank to cash a cheque.

"Good morning", says Ed, "could you please cash this cheque for me?"

Cashier: "It would be my pleasure Sir, but could you please show me some identification?"

Miliband: "Truthfully. I did not bring my ID with me as I didn't think there was any need to. But hang on! I'm Ed Miliband, Leader of the Opposition and of the Labour Party!!!"

Cashier: "Yes Sir, I know who you are, but with all the regulations and monitoring of the banks because of impostors and forgers etc., I must insist on seeing some identification."

Miliband: "Just ask any of the customers here at the bank who I am and they will tell you. Everybody knows who I am!"

Cashier: "I'm sorry Sir, but these are the bank rules and I must follow them."

☞ ☞ ☞

Miliband: "I am urging you please, to cash this cheque for me."

Cashier: "Look Sir, this is what we can do. One day Rory McIlroy came into the bank without any ID. To prove he was Rory McIlroy he pulled out his putter and putted a ball along the floor and into a small cup. With that sort of skill we knew it was Rory McIlroy and we cashed his cheque. On another occasion, Andy Murray came in without any ID. He pulled out his tennis racquet and lobbed a tennis ball straight into my teacup with such a spectacular shot that we all knew it was Andy Murray.

Ed Miliband stood there thinking and thinking and then finally says, "To be honest, there is nothing that comes to my mind. I can't think of a single thing that I'm any good at."

Cashier: "Will it be large or small notes you require Mr Miliband ?

☺   ☺   ☺

Two Inuit (eskimos) sitting in a kayak were chilly, so they lit a fire in the craft. Unsurprisingly it sank, proving once again that you can't have your kayak and heat it too.

Turning the Tables on a Bank

We believe this to be an actual letter sent to a bank in the United States. It is thought to have been published in the New York Times.

Dear Sir,

I am writing to thank you for bouncing the check with which I endeavoured to pay my plumber last month. By my calculations some three nanoseconds must have elapsed between his presenting the check, and the arrival in my account of the funds needed to honor it. I refer, of course, to the automatic monthly deposit of my entire salary, an arrangement which, I admit, has only been in place for eight years.

You are to be commended for seizing that brief window of opportunity, and also for debiting my account with $50 by way of penalty for the inconvenience I caused to your bank. My thankfulness springs from the manner in which this incident has caused me to rethink my errant financial ways.

You have set me on the path of fiscal righteousness. No more will our relationship be blighted by these unpleasant incidents, as I am

☞ ☞ ☞

restructuring my affairs as from 1 Jjanuary next year, taking as my model the procedures, attitudes and conduct of your very bank. I can think of no greater compliment, and I know you will be excited and proud to hear it. To this end, please be advised about the following changes:

1) I have noticed that whereas I personally attend to your telephone calls and letters, when I try to contact you I am confronted by the impersonal, ever-changing, pre-recorded, faceless entity which your bank has become. From now on I, like you, choose only to deal with a flesh and blood person. My mortgage and loan repayments will, therefore and hereafter, no longer be automatic, but will arrive at your bank, by check, addressed personally and confidentially to an employee of your branch, whom you must nominate. You will be aware that it is an offense under the Postal Act for any other person to open such an envelope.

2) Please find attached an Application for Authorized Contact Status which your chosen employee is required to complete. I am sorry it runs to eight pages, but in order that I know as much about him or her as your bank knows about me, there is no alternative. Please note that all copies of his or her medical history must be countersigned by a Justice of the Peace, and that

☞ ☞ ☞

the mandatory details of his/her financial situation (income, debts, assets and liabilities) must be accompanied by documented proof. In due course I will issue your employee with a PIN number which he/she must quote in all dealings with me. I regret that it cannot be shorter than 28 digits but, again, I have modelled it on the number of button presses required to access my account balance on your phone bank service. As they say, imitation is the sincerest form of flattery.

3) Let me level the playing field even further by introducing you to my new telephone system, which you will notice, is very much like yours. My Authorized Contact at your bank, the only person with whom I will have any dealings, may call me at any time and will be answered by an automated voice. Press buttons as follows:

1 To make an appointment to see me.

2 To query a missing payment.

3 To transfer the call to my living room in case I am there.

4 To transfer the call to my bedroom in case I am sleeping.

5 To transfer the call to my toilet in case I am attending to nature.

6 To transfer the call to my mobile phone in case I am not at home.

☞ ☞ ☞

7   To leave a message on my computer [to leave a
    message a password to access my computer is
    required: password will be communicated at a
    later date to the Authorized Contact]
8   To return to the main menu and listen carefully
    to options 1 through 7
9   To make a general complaint or inquiry. The
    Authorized Contact will then be put on hold,
    pending the attention of my automated
    answering service.

While this may on occasion involve a lengthy wait,
uplifting music will play for the duration. This
month I've chosen a refrain from "The Best of
Woody Guthrie":

> "Oh, the banks are made of marble,
> With a guard at every door,
> And the vaults are filled with silver,
> That the miners sweated for."

After twenty minutes of that, our mutual Contact
will probably know it by heart.

4) On a more serious note, we come to the matter
of cost. As your bank has often pointed out, the
ongoing drive for greater efficiency comes at a
cost, a cost which you have always been quick to
pass on to me.

☞ ☞ ☞

Let me repay your kindness by passing some costs back. First, there is the matter of advertising material you send me. This I will read for a fee of $20 per page. Inquiries from your Authorized Contact will be billed at $5 per minute of my time spent in response. Any debits to my account, as, for example, in the matter of the penalty for the dishonoured check, will be passed back to you. My new phone service runs at 75 cents a minute (even Woody Guthrie doesn't come for free), so you would be well advised to keep your inquiries brief and to the point.

5) Regrettably, but again following your example, I must also levy an establishment fee of 2% of my balance or $50 (whichever is more) to cover the setting up of this new arrangement.

May I wish you a happy, if ever-so-slightly less prosperous, New Year.

Your humble client,

Jules Winder

Me and 18 of me mates went to the cinema. The ticket lady asks "Why so many of you?" So I says, "The film said 18 or over."

The Jigsaw

A girl calls her boyfriend and says, "Please come over here and help me. I have this killer jigsaw puzzle and I can't figure out how to get it started."

Her boyfriend asks, "What is it supposed to be when it's finished?" The girlfriend says, "According to the picture on the box, it's a tiger."

Her boyfriend decides to go over and help her with the puzzle. She lets him in and shows him where she has the puzzle spread all over the table.

He studies the pieces for a moment, then looks at the box, then turns to her and says: "First of all, no matter what we do, we're not going to be able to assemble these pieces into anything resembling a tiger. Second, I'd advise you to relax. Let's have a cup of coffee, then....we'll put all the frosted flakes back in the box."

☺   ☺   ☺

When I was in the pub I heard a couple of plonkers saying that they wouldn't feel safe on an aircraft if they knew the pilot was a woman. What a pair of sexists! I mean, it's not as if she'd have to reverse the thing!

Axes of Evil and Just as Evil and Nearly Evil

Beijing (SatireWire.com) - Bitter after being snubbed for membership in the "Axis of Evil", Libya, China, and Syria today announced they had formed the **"Axis of Just as Evil,"** which they said would be way eviler than that stupid Iran-Iraq-North Korea axis President Bush warned of in his State of the Union address.

Axis of Evil members, however, immediately dismissed the new axis as having, for starters, a really dumb name. "Right. They are Just as Evil... in their dreams!" declared North Korean leader Kim Jong-il. "Everybody knows we're the best evils... best at being evil... we're the best."

Diplomats from Syria denied they were jealous about being excluded, although they conceded they did ask if they could join the Axis of Evil. "They told us it was full," said Syrian President Bashar al-Assad. "An Axis can't have more than three countries," explained Iraqi President Saddam Hussein. "This is not my rule, it's tradition. In World War II you had Germany, Italy, and Japan in the evil Axis. So you can only have three. And a secret handshake. Ours is wicked cool."

☞ ☞ ☞

The axis pandemic

International reaction to Bush's Axis of Evil declaration was swift, as within minutes, France surrendered.

Elsewhere, peer-conscious nations rushed to gain triumvirate status in what became a game of geopolitical chairs. Cuba, Sudan, and Serbia said they had formed the **Axis of Somewhat Evil**, forcing Somalia to join with Uganda and Myanmar in the **Axis of Occasionally Evil**, while Bulgaria, Indonesia and Russia established the **Axis of Not So Much Evil As Just Generally Disagreeable**.

With the criteria suddenly expanded and all the desirable clubs filling up, Sierra Leone, El Salvador, and Rwanda applied to be called the **Axis of Countries That Aren't the Worst But Certainly Won't Be Asked to Host the Olympics.**

Canada, Mexico, and Australia formed the **Axis of Nations That Are Actually Quite Nice But Secretly Have Nasty Thoughts About America**, while Spain, Scotland, and New Zealand established the **Axis of Countries That Be Allowed to Ask Sheep to Wear Lipstick**. "That's not a threat, really, just something we like to do,"

☞ ☞ ☞

said Scottish Executive First Minister Jack McConnell.

While wondering if the other nations of the world weren't perhaps making fun of him, a cautious Bush granted approval for most axes, although he rejected the establishment of the **Axis of Countries Whose Names End in "Guay,"** accusing one of its members of filing a false application. Officials from Paraguay, Uruguay, and Chadguay denied the charges.

Israel, meanwhile, insisted it didn't want to join any Axis, but privately, world leaders said that's only because no one asked them.

☺   ☺   ☺

Nearly a Police Arrest

Two policemen (Constable Ken and Bob) call the station on the radio. "Hello. Is that the Sarge?"
"Yes?" comes the reply

"We have a case here. A woman has shot her husband for stepping on the floor she had just mopped clean."
"Have you arrested the woman?"

"No sir. The floor is still wet."

Walking on Water

Joe had long heard the stories of an amazing family tradition. It seems that his father, grandfather and great-grandfather had all been able to walk on water on their 18th birthday. On that special day, they had each walked across the lake to the pub on the far side for their first legal drink.

So, when Joe's 18th birthday came around, he and his pal, Mick, took a boat out to the middle of the lake. Joe stepped out of the boat and nearly drowned! Mick barely managed to pull him to safety.

Furious and confused, Joe went to see his grandmother. "Grandma," he asked, "it's my 18th birthday, so why can't I walk across the lake like my father, his father and his father before him?" Granny looked deeply into Joe's troubled brown eyes and said: "Because your father, your grandfather and your great grandfather were all born in December, when the lake is frozen; and you were born in August."

☺   ☺   ☺

Why do croutons come in airtight packages? Aren't they just stale bread to begin with?.

Police Complaint

The following is a complaint was reportedly sent to a police station (*names changed by editors*):

Dear Sir/Madam/Automated telephone answering service,

Having spent the past twenty minutes waiting for someone at Greewick police station to pick up a telephone I have decided to abandon the idea and try e-mailing you instead.

Perhaps you would be so kind as to pass this message on to your colleagues in Greewick, by means of smoke signal, carrier pigeon or ouija board.

As I'm writing this e-mail there are eleven failed medical experiments (I think you call them youths) in Mathie Crescent, which is just off Mathie Road in Blackfern.

Six of them seem happy enough to play a game which involves kicking a football against an iron gate with the force of a meteorite. This causes an earth shattering CLANG! which rings throughout the entire building. This game is now in its third week and as I am unsure how the scoring system works, I have no idea if it will end any time soon.

☞ ☞ ☞

The remaining five wastes of space are happily rummaging through several bags of rubbish and items of furniture that someone has so thoughtfully dumped beside the rubbish bins. One of them has found a saw and is setting about a discarded chair like a beaver on ecstasy pills.

I fear that it's only a matter of time before they turn their limited attention to the gas bottle that is lying between the two bins. If they could be relied on to only to injure themselves then I would happily leave them to it and even go so far as to lend them the matches. Unfortunately they are far more likely to blow up half the street with them and I've just finished decorating my kitchen.

What I suggest is this: after replying to this e-mail with worthless assurances that the matter is being looked into and will be dealt with, why not leave it until the one night of the year (probably bath night) when there are no mutants around then drive up the street in a police car before doing a three point turn and disappearing again. This will of course serve no other purpose than to remind us what policemen actually look like.

I trust that when I take a claw hammer to the skull of one of these throwbacks you'll do me the same courtesy of giving me a four month head start before coming to arrest me.

☞ ☞ ☞

I remain your obedient servant

Annoyed Citizen

To which the replay was:

Dear Annoyed Citizen,

I have read your e-mail and understand your frustration at the problems caused by youths playing in the area and the problems you have encountered in trying to contact the police.

As the Community Officer for your street I would like to extend an offer to discuss the matter fully with you. Should you wish to discuss the matter, please provide contact details (address / telephone number) and when may be suitable.

Regards

PC Plod
Community Officer

☺   ☺   ☺

Two hydrogen atoms meet. One says, 'I've lost my electron.' The other says, ' Are you sure?' The first replies, 'Yes, I'm positive.'

The Artist

Billy Joe Bob, while not a brilliant scholar, was a gifted portrait artist. His fame grew and soon people from all over the country were coming to him for paintings.

One day, a beautiful young woman pulled up to his house in a stretch limo. She asked Billy Joe Bob if he would paint her in the nude. This was the first time anyone had made this request, but the beautiful lady said money was no object and that she was willing to pay $50,000 for the painting.

Not wanting to get into trouble with Bobbie Sue, his wife and cousin, Billy Joe Bob asked the lady to wait while he went into the house and conferred with Bobbie Sue.

In a few minutes he returned and told the lady he was willing to do it... however, he would have to leave his socks on so he would have some place to wipe his brushes.

☺   ☺   ☺

A hole has been found in the nudist-camp wall. The police are looking into it.

Spare a Thought for Michael O'Leary, CEO of 'Ryanair' (famous low cost airline)

Arriving in a hotel in Dublin, Michael went to the bar and asked for a pint of draught Guinness. The barman nodded and said, "That will be one Euro please, Mr. O'Leary."

Somewhat taken aback, O'Leary replied: "That's very cheap" and handed over his money.

"Well, we try to stay ahead of the competition", said the barman. "And we are serving free pints every Wednesday evening from 6 until 8. We have the cheapest beer in Ireland."

"That is remarkable value" Michael comments. The barman replies: "I see you don't seem to have a glass, so you'll probably need one of ours - That will be 3 Euro please."

O'Leary scowled, but paid up. He took his drink and walked towards a seat.

"Ah, you want to sit down?" said the barman. "That'll be an extra 2 Euro. You could have pre-booked the seat, and it would have only cost you one Euro."

☞ ☞ ☞

"I think you may to be too big for the seat sir, can I ask you to sit in this frame please"

Michael attempts to sit down but the frame is too small and when he can't squeeze in he complains "Nobody would fit in that little frame".
"I'm afraid if you can't fit in the frame you'll have to pay an extra surcharge of 4 Euro for your seat sir"

O'Leary swore to himself, but paid up. "I see that you have brought your laptop with you" added the barman. "And since that wasn't pre-booked either, that will be another 3 Euro."

O'Leary was so annoyed that he walked back to the bar, slammed his drink on the counter, and yelled, "This is ridiculous, I want to speak to the manager."

"Ah, I see you want to use the counter" says the barman, "that will be 2 Euro please." O'Leary's face was red with rage. "Do you know who I am?" he shouts.

"Of course I do Mr. O'Leary,"

"I've had enough, What sort of hotel is this? I come in for a quiet drink and you treat me like this. I insist on speaking to a manager!"

☞ ☞ ☞

"Here is his e-mail address, or if you wish, you can contact him between 9 and 9.10 every morning, Monday to Tuesday at this free phone number. Calls are free, until they are answered, then there is a talking charge of only 10 cent per second."

"I will never use this bar again."

"OK sir, but remember, we are the only hotel in Ireland selling pints for one Euro."

☺   ☺   ☺

How to Sex Flies

A woman walked into her kitchen to find her husband stalking around with a fly swatter.

"What are you doing?" she asked.
"Killing flies." he answered.

"Have you got any yet?" she enquired.
"Yes," he replied, "three male and two female."

"How do you know whether they are male or female" she asked.

"3 were on the beer can and 2 on the phone" he replied.

Eye Catching

A man is dining in a fancy restaurant. He has been check out the gorgeous redhead sitting at the next table but lacks the nerve to talk with her.

Suddenly she sneezes, and her glass eye comes flying out of its socket towards the man. He reflexively reaches out, grabs it out of the air, and hands it back to her.

"Oh, I am so sorry," the woman says as she pops her eye back in place. "Please let me buy your dinner to make it up to you," she says.

They enjoy a wonderful dinner together, and afterwards they go to the theatre followed by drinks. They talk, they laugh, she shares her deepest dreams and he shares his. They listen to each other entranced.

They have a wonderful, wonderful time and meet every day for the next week, romance blossoming.

"You know," he says, "you are the perfect woman. Are you this nice to every guy you meet?"

"No," she replies........." you just happened to catch my eye."

 ☺   ☺   ☺

Depressed Man Diagnosed as "British"

George Farthing, an expatriate British man living in America, was recently diagnosed as clinically depressed, tanked up on anti-depressants and scheduled for controversial shock therapy when doctors realised he wasn't depressed at all - only British.

Mr. Farthing, a British man whose characteristic pessimism and gloomy perspective were interpreted as serious clinical depression, was led on a nightmare journey through the American psychiatric system. Doctors described Farthing as suffering with pervasive negative anticipation - a belief that everything will turn out for the worst, whether it's trains arriving late, England's chances at winning any international sports event or even his own prospects to get ahead in life and achieve his dreams. "The satisfaction Mr. Farthing seemed to get from his pessimism seemed particularly pathological" reported the doctors. "They put me on everything - lithium, prozac, St. John's wort," said Mr. Farthing. "They even told me to sit in front of a big light for an hour a day or I'd become suicidal. I kept telling them that this was all pointless and they said that it was exactly that sort of attitude that got me here in the first place."

☞ ☞ ☞

Running out of ideas, his doctors finally resorted to a course of 'weapons grade MDMA', the only noticeable effect of which was six hours of speedy repetitions of the phrases "mustn't grumble" and "not too bad, really". It was then that Mr. Farthing was referred to a psychotherapist.

Dr. Isaac Horney explored Mr. Farthing's family history and couldn't believe his ears. "His story of a childhood growing up in a gray little town where it rained every day, treeless streets of identical houses and passionately backing a football team who never won seemed to be typical depressive ideation or false memory. Mr Farthing had six months of therapy but seemed to mainly want to talk about the weather - how miserable and cold it was in winter and later how difficult and hot it is in summer. I felt he wasn't responding to therapy at all and so I recommended drastic action namely ECT or shock treatment".

"I was all prepared & secured down on the table and they were about to put the rubber bit in my mouth when the psychiatric nurse picked up on my accent." said Mr. Farthing. "I remember her saying 'oh my god, I think we're making a terrible mistake'." Nurse Alice Sheen was a big fan of British comedy giving her an understanding of the British psyche.

☞ ☞ ☞

"Classic comedy characters like Tony Hancock, Albert Steptoe and Frank Spencer are all hopeless cases with no chance of ever doing well or escaping their circumstances," she explained to the baffled U.S. medics. "That's funny in Britain and is not seen as pathological at all."

Identifying Mr. Farthing as British changed this diagnosis from 'clinical depression' to 'rather quaint and charming' and he was immediately discharged from hospital, with a selection of brightly coloured leaflets and an "I Love New York" T-shirt.

☺   ☺   ☺

More Police Quotes

"If you take your hands off the car, I'll make your birth certificate a worthless document."

"You don't know how fast you were going? I guess that means I can write anything I want to on the ticket, huh?"

"Just how big were those 'two beers' you say you had?"

"Yeah, we have a quota. Two more tickets and my wife gets a toaster oven."

The Deaf Drunk.

A man who has had a little too much to drink is driving home from the city one night and, of course, his car is weaving violently all over the road.

A cop pulls him over. "So," says the cop to the driver, "where have ya been?" "Why, I've been to the pub of course." slurs the drunk.

"Well," says the cop, "it looks like you've had quite a few to drink this evening." "I did all right," the drunk says with a smile. "Did you know" says the cop, standing straight and folding his arms across his chest, "that a few intersections back, your wife fell out of your car?"

"Oh, thank heavens," sighs the drunk. "For a minute there, I thought I'd gone deaf."

☺   ☺   ☺

I live in a semi-rural area. We recently had a new neighbor call the local township administrative office to request the removal of the Deer Crossing sign on our road. The reason: too many deer were being hit by cars and he didn't want them to cross there anymore.

Terrorism Alert!

The British have reacted to the recent terrorism alerts by raising their security level from "Miffed" to "Peeved." Soon, though, security levels may be raised yet again to "Irritated" or even "A Bit Cross."

Londoners have not been "A Bit Cross" since the blitz in 1940, when tea supplies all but ran out.

Terrorists have been re-categorized from "Tiresome" to a "Bloody Nuisance." The last time the British issued a "Bloody Nuisance" warning level was during the great fire of 1666.

Also, the French Government announced yesterday that it has raised its terror alert level from "Run" to "Hide."

The only two higher levels in France are "Surrender" and "Collaborate." The rise was precipitated by a recent fire that destroyed France's white flag factory, effectively paralyzing the country's military capability.

It's not only the English and French that are on a heightened level of alert. Italy has increased the alert level from "Shout Loudly and Excitedly" to "Elaborate Military Posturing." Two more levels remain: "Ineffective Combat Operations" and "Change Sides."

The Germans also increased their alert state from "Disdainful Arrogance" to "Sing Marching Songs". They also have two higher levels: "Invade a Neighbour" and "Lose."

Belgians, on the other hand, are all on holiday, as is customary. The only threat they are worried about is NATO pulling out of Brussels.

Meanwhile, in the Southern hemisphere:

New Zealand has also raised its security levels - from "baaa" to "BAAAA!" Due to continuing defense cutbacks (the air force being a squadron of spotty teenagers flying paper aeroplanes and the navy some toy boats in the Prime Minister's bath), New Zealand only has one more level of escalation, which is "I hope Australia will come to rescue us". In the event of invasion, New Zealanders will be asked to gather together in a strategic defensive position, called Bondi.

(It might be worth noting that New Zealand would be unable to raise an army as its soldiers are all currently deployed playing orcs in the upcoming Hobbit movie.)

☞ ☞ ☞

Australia, meanwhile, has raised its security level from "No worries" to "She'll be right, mate". Three more escalation levels remain: "Crikey!, I think we'll need to cancel the barbie this weekend" and "The barbie is cancelled." It should be noted that there has not been a situation yet that has warranted the use of the final escalation level.

"European Terror Alerts" joke - Unknown origin, forwarded around as a chain mail during 2010. In some versions of this email (and there many) John Cleese is cited as the author. This is, of course, intended to be humorous - so please hold back troop deployments for now.

☺   ☺   ☺

Calling 999

A man is cleaning his rifle and accidentally shoots his wife. He immediately dials 999 and hysterically shrieks down the phone: "It's my wife! I've accidentally shot her, I've killed her!"

Operator: "Please calm down Sir. Can you first make sure she is actually dead!"

click..... *BANG*

Man: "OK, I've done that. What next?"

Driving on the Motorway

This morning, on the motorway, I looked over to my right and there was a woman in a brand new BMW doing 75mph! With her face up next to her rear view mirror!! Putting on her eyeliner!!!

I looked away for a couple of seconds and when I looked back she was halfway over in my lane, still working on that makeup.

As a man, I don't scare easily, but she scared me so much that I dropped my electric shaver, which knocked the meat pie out of my other hand. In all the confusion of trying to straighten out the car, using my knees against the steering wheel, my mobile phone got knocked away from my ear, which fell into the coffee between my legs, which, soaked my trousers and burned my legs, ruined the phone and disconnected an important call.

Women drivers!!!

Two silk worms had a race. They ended up in a tie.

I planted some bird seed. A bird came up.
Now I don't know what to feed it.

This page is for all the jokes you've just remembered

2 FOR TRAVELERS EVERYWHERE

These announcements are dedicated to all the travelers...
They have been attributed to many different airlines and we
have been unable to verify any individual one.

Checking in

I was at the airport, checking in at the gate when an airport employee asked: "Has anyone put anything in your baggage without your knowledge?" To which I replied, "If it was without my knowledge, how would I know?"

Pre-take Off Announcements

"In the event of a sudden loss of cabin pressure, masks will descend from the ceiling. Stop screaming, grab the mask, and pull it over your face. If you have a small child traveling with you, secure your mask before assisting with theirs. If you are traveling with more than one small child, pick your favorite."

"Weather at our destination is 50 degrees with some broken clouds, but we'll try to have them fixed before we arrive. Thank you, and remember, nobody loves you, or your money, more than Southwest Airlines."

☞ ☞ ☞

On a flight, where there is no assigned seating, and you can sit where you want, passengers were apparently having a hard time choosing, when a flight attendant announced: "People, people we're not picking out furniture here, find a seat and get in it!"

From a flight attendant: "Welcome aboard flight 271 to Port Elizabeth. To operate your seat belt, insert the metal tab into the buckle, and pull tight. It works just like every other seat belt; and, if you don't know how to operate one, you probably shouldn't be out in public unsupervised."

"Your seat cushions can be used for flotation and in the event of an emergency water landing, please paddle to shore and keep them with our compliments."

And from the pilot during his welcome message: "We are pleased to announce that we have some of the best flight attendants in the industry. Unfortunately, none of them are on this flight!"

"There may be 50 ways to leave your lover, but there are only 4 ways out of this airplane."

"Thank you for flying with us. We hope you enjoyed giving us the business as much as we enjoyed taking you for a ride."

☞ ☞ ☞

Heard on a flight. "Ladies and gentlemen, if you wish to smoke, the smoking section on this airplane is on the wing. If you can light 'em, you can smoke 'em."

In-flight announcement

A plane was taking off from Kennedy International Airport in New York. After it reached a comfortable cruising altitude, the captain announced over the intercom: "Ladies and gentlemen, this is your captain speaking. Welcome to Flight Number 293, non-stop from New York to Los Angeles.

The weather ahead is good and, therefore, we should have a smooth and uneventful flight. Now sit back and relax... OH, MY GOD!"

Silence followed, and after a few minutes, the captain came back on the intercom and said, "Ladies and Gentlemen, I am so sorry if I scared you earlier. While I was talking to you, the flight attendant accidentally spilled a cup of hot coffee in my lap. You should see the front of my pants!" A passenger in Coach yelled, "That's nothing. You should see the back of mine!"

☺   ☺   ☺

On one flight the pilot announced over the PA system: "Ladies and gentlemen, we've reached cruising altitude and will be turning down the cabin lights. This is for your comfort and to enhance the appearance of your flight attendants."

Landing announcements

An airline pilot wrote that on this particular flight he had hammered his ship into the runway really hard. The airline had a policy which required the first officer to stand at the door while the passengers exited, smile, and give them a "Thanks for flying our airline." He said that, in light of his bad landing, he had a hard time looking the passengers in the eye, thinking that someone would have a smart comment.

Finally everyone had gotten off except for a little old lady walking with a cane. She said: "Sir, do you mind if I ask you a question?"

"Why, no Ma'am," said the pilot. "What is it?"
The little old lady said: "Did we land, or were we shot down?"

☺   ☺   ☺

As the plane landed and was coming to a stop at a major international airport, a lone voice came over the loudspeaker: "Whoa, big fella. WHOA!"

On landing, the stewardess said: "Please be sure to take all of your belongings. If you're going to leave anything, please make sure it's something we'd like to have."

Another flight attendant's comment on a less than perfect landing: "We ask you to please remain seated as Captain Kangaroo bounces us to the terminal."

Heard on flight 255 just after a very hard landing: The flight attendant came on the intercom and said, "That was quite a bump and I know what y'all are thinking. I'm here to tell you it wasn't the airline's fault, it wasn't the pilot's fault, it wasn't the flight attendant's fault, it was the asphalt."

"As you exit the plane, make sure to gather all of your belongings. Anything left behind will be distributed evenly among the flight attendants. Please do not leave children or spouses."

Overheard on a Kulula flight into Cape Town, on a particularly windy and bumpy day: During the final approach, the Captain really had to fight it.

☞ ☞ ☞

After an extremely hard landing, the Flight Attendant said, "Ladies and Gentlemen, welcome to The Mother City. Please remain in your seats with your seat belts fastened while the Captain taxis what's left of our airplane to the gate!"

After a particularly rough landing during thunderstorms, a flight attendant announced: "Please take care when opening the overhead compartments because, after a landing like that, sure as hell everything has shifted."

After a real crusher of a landing, the attendant came on with, "Ladies and Gentlemen, please remain in your seats until Captain Crash and the crew have brought the aircraft to a screeching halt against the gate. And, once the tire smoke has cleared and the warning bells are silenced, we will open the door and you can pick your way through the wreckage to the terminal."

Part of a flight attendant's arrival announcement: "We'd like to thank you folks for flying with us today. And, the next time you get the insane urge to go blasting through the skies in a pressurized metal tube, we hope you'll think of our airline."

At the Border Checkpoint

Five Englishmen in an Audi Quattro arrived at an border checkpoint. The officer, stops them and tells them: "It is illegal to put five people in a Quattro. Quattro means four."

"Quattro is just the name of the automobile," the Englishman retorted disbelievingly. "Look at the papers: this car is designed to carry five persons."

"You cannot pull that one on me," replies the officer. "Quattro means four. You have five people in your car and you are therefore breaking the law."

"You idiot!" the Englishmen replies angrily. "Call your supervisor over. I want to speak to someone with more intelligence!"

"Sorry" responds the office, "my supervisor is busy with two people in a Fiat Uno."

☺   ☺   ☺

Sign in a cocktail lounge, Norway: 'Ladies are requested not to have children in the bar.'

Sign in a doctor's office, Rome: 'Specialist in women and other diseases'.

Southwest Airlines

A passenger recorded this pre-flight announcement on Southwest Airlines. It certainly grabbed the attention of the passengers.... The stewardess was later interviewed on the USA television show 'Ellen'.

"I'd like to pretend to have your attention for just a few moments.

My ex-husband, my new boyfriend and our divorce attorney are gonna show you the safety features on this 737 – 800 series.

It's been a long day for me.

To properly fasten your seatbelt slide the flat end in the buckle. To release, lift up on the buckle.

Position your seatbelt tight and low across your hips like my grandmother wears her support bra.

If you get mad and want to take your toys and go home there's six ways to get there. Two forward exit doors, two over wing exits, two rear exits. There are signs overhead and lights on each floor near each exit.

Everybody gets a door prize. In the seatback pocket in front of you, along with dirty diapers,

☞ ☞ ☞

chewing gum wrappers, banana peels and all other gifts you leave for us, right on top is a safety information card. Take it out, check it out.

You will notice in the highly unlikely event that the captain lands us near a hot tub everybody gets their own teeny-weeny yellow Southwest bikini. One size fits all. Take it out only when told to do so. Place it over your head, put that strap around your waist, buckle it in front, pull it tight and, once outside, pull the red tab to inflate.

My attendants are coming by hoping you tell them how good-looking they are. They're gonna make sure your seat backs and tray tables are in their full upright and absolutely most uncomfortable position possible. And that your carry on items are crammed in the overhead storage or shoved completely under the seat in front of you leaving absolutely no room for your knees or feet.

As you know, it's a no smoking, no whining no complaining flight. It's a "please" and "thank you" and "you are such a good-looking flight attendant" flight.

Smoking is never allowed on board at Southwest. If you are caught smoking in a lavatory the fine for that is $2000. If you wanted to pay that for your airfare you should have flown somebody else.

☞ ☞ ☞

If we do make you feel that nervous in the next hour and a half, you're more than welcome to step outside. We don't discriminate at Southwest we have a special smoking section just for you. We will even show you a movie tonight. We have "Up in the Air." And the flight attendant serving you is Wendy and her motto is "if you can light it, you can smoke it". It's against the law to tamper or disable any smoke detector in the lavatory. Federal aviation regulations about passenger compliance are on passenger information signs and posted on placards. Basically, just do what we say and nobody gets hurt.

And although we never anticipate a loss in cabin pressure – if we did we certainly wouldn't be at work tonight. But if needed, oxygen masks come out of the compartment overhead. Stop screaming, let go of your neighbour, pull until that plastic tubing is fully extended, place the mask over your nose and mouth and breathe normally. To activate the flow of oxygen simply insert $.75 for the first minute and $.50 for each additional minute. Although that plastic bag may not inflate, you are receiving lots of gin, oxygen that is. And if you're travelling with small children… we're sorry. If you're travelling with more than one child, pick out the one who you think might have the most earning potential down the road and if you're travelling with somebody needing special assistance – like your husband, bless his heart, or your wife - put on your mask first.

That's it for the dos and don'ts of show and tell. So, sit back and relax or you can sit up and be tense. Either way it's a one and a half hour flight gate to gate and the clock 's already ticking.

Seriously, if there is anything at all we can do to make your flight more enjoyable please tell us... just as soon as we land in Salt Lake City.

And if there's anything you can do to make our flight more enjoyable we'll tell you immediately. We're not shy on Southwest.

That's what we call very cheap entertainment. Nobody had to pay extra but you certainly don't get a refund. Thank you for choosing Southwest, welcome aboard!

☺   ☺   ☺

Been Everywhere.... Done Everything

An Asian fellow has moved in next door. He has travelled the world, swum with sharks, wrestled bears and climbed the highest mountains. It came as no surprise to learn his name was Bindair Dundat.

In a Game Park...

A wealthy old lady decides to go on a photo safari in Africa, taking her faithful aged poodle named Cuddles, along for the company.

One day the poodle starts chasing butterflies and before long, Cuddles discovers that she's lost. Wandering about, she notices a leopard heading rapidly in her direction with the intention of having lunch.

The old poodle thinks, "Oh, oh! I'm in deep doo-doo now!" Noticing some bones on the ground close by, she immediately settles down to chew on the bones with her back to the approaching cat.

Just as the leopard is about to leap, the old poodle exclaims loudly, "Boy, that was one delicious leopard! I wonder if there are any more around here?"

Hearing this, the young leopard halts his attack in mid-strike, a look of terror comes over him and he slinks away into the trees. "Whew!", says the leopard, "That was close! That old poodle nearly had me!"

Meanwhile, a monkey who had been watching the whole scene from a nearby tree, figures he can put

☞   ☞   ☞

this knowledge to good use and trade it for protection from the leopard. So off he goes, but the old poodle sees him heading after the leopard with great speed, and figures that something must be up. The monkey soon catches up with the leopard, spills the beans and strikes a deal for himself with the leopard.

The young leopard is furious at being made a fool of and says, "Here, monkey, hop on my back and see what's going to happen to that conniving canine!"

Now, the old poodle sees the leopard coming with the monkey on his back and thinks, "What am I going to do now?", but instead of running, the dog sits down with her back to her attackers, pretending she hasn't seen them yet, and just when they get close enough to hear, the old poodle says: "Where's that damn monkey? I sent him off an hour ago to bring me another leopard!"

Moral of this story... Don't mess with old geezers... age and treachery will always overcome youth and skill! Wisdom and brilliance only come with age and experience!

☺   ☺   ☺

Jokes about German sausages are the wurst.

Heard on the London Underground

These announcements were heard on the London Underground (subway) and reputedly collected by Annie Mole. While additional actual announcements are reportedly available on her website, we were unable to locate that site.

"Ladies and Gentlemen, I do apologize for the delay to your service. I know you're all dying to get home, unless, of course, you happen to be married to my ex-wife, in which case you'll want to cross over to the Westbound and go in the opposite direction."

"Your delay this evening is caused by the line controller suffering from E & B syndrome: not knowing his elbow from his backside. I'll let you know any further information as soon as I'm given any."

"Do you want the good news first or the bad news? The good news is that last Friday was my birthday and I hit the town and had a great time. The bad news is that there is a points failure somewhere between Mile End and East Ham, which means we probably won't reach our destination."

☞ ☞ ☞

"Let the passengers off the train FIRST!' (Pause) Oh go on then, stuff yourselves in like sardines, see if I care. I'm going home..."

"Ladies and gentlemen, we apologize for the delay, but there is a security alert at Victoria station and we are therefore stuck here for the foreseeable future, so let's take our minds off it and pass some time together. All together now.... 'Ten green bottles, hanging on a wall...'."

"We are now travelling through Baker Street station... As you can see, Baker Street station is closed. It would have been nice if they had actually told me, so I could have told you earlier, but no, they don't think about things like that."

During an extremely hot rush hour on the Central Line, the driver announced in a West Indian drawl: "Step right this way for the sauna, ladies and gentleman... unfortunately, towels are not provided."

"Please allow the doors to close. Try not to confuse this with 'Please hold the doors open.' The two are distinct and separate instructions. Please note that the beeping noise coming from the doors means that the doors are about to close. It does not mean throw yourself or your bags into the doors."

☞ ☞ ☞

"We can't move off because some idiot has their hand stuck in the door."

"To the gentleman wearing the long grey coat trying to get on the second carriage -- what part of 'stand clear of the doors' don't you understand?"

"Please move all baggage away from the doors." (Pause...) "Please move ALL belongings away from the doors." (Pause...) "This is a personal message to the man in the brown suit wearing glasses at the rear of the train: Put the pie down, and move your golf clubs away from the door"

"May I remind all passengers that there is strictly no smoking allowed on any part of the Underground. However, if you are smoking a joint, it's only fair that you pass it round the rest of the carriage."

"Beggars are operating on this train. Please do NOT encourage these professional beggars. If you have any spare change, please give it to a registered charity. Failing that, give it to me."

"The future will be better tomorrow."

Chinese for Beginners

When you travel to a foreign country it is always useful to have a few handy phrases up your sleeve. These Chinese phrases may be of use... on the other hand they may not!

That's not right.	Sum Ting Wong
Are you harboring a fugitive?	Hu Yu Hai Ding?
See me ASAP.	Kum Hia Nao
Stupid Man.	Dum Gai
Small Horse.	Tai Ni Po Ni
Did you go to the beach?	Wai Yu So Tan?
I bumped into a coffee table.	Ai Bang Mai Ni
I think you need a face lift.	Chin Tu Fat
It's very dark in here.	Wai So Dim?
I thought you were on a diet.	Wai Yu Mun Ching?
This is a tow away zone.	No Pah King
Our meeting is scheduled for next week.	
	Wai Yu Kum Nao?
Staying out of sight.	Lei Ying Lo
He's cleaning his automobile.	Wa Shing Ka
Great!	Su Pah

Signs Seen Around the World

Dry cleaners, Bangkok: 'Drop your trousers here for the best results'.

On an automatic restroom hand dryer: 'do not activate with wet hands.'

This page is for all the funny announcements
you have heard.

3 DID HE *REALLY* SAY THAT???

Quotes, whether from children, famous people or anyone in between are often amusing - or ironically true.

Editors

Famous Football Quotes

These quotes have been attributed to both Ron Atkinson (former Manchester United manager turned soccer expert on British TV) and Kevin Keegan (former football player and manager of the England World Cup team). We have not been able to verify which of them (if either) actually made these statements.

"He can't speak Turks, but you can tell he's delighted."

"The 33 or 34-year-olds will be 36 or 37 by the time the next World Cup comes around, if they're not careful."

"There'll be no siestas in Madrid tonight."

"They compare Steve McManaman to Steve Heighway and he's nothing like him, but I can see why - it's because he's a bit different. They both called Steve."

"Despite his white boots, he has real pace and aggression."

"Goalkeepers aren't born today until they're in their late 20s or 30s and sometimes not even then. Or so it would appear. To me anyway. Don't you think the same?"

"The substitute is about to come on - he's a player who was left out of the starting line-up today. There were others as well."

"Chile have three options - they could win or they could lose. It's up to them, the tide is in their court now."

"England have the best fans in the world and Scotland's fans are second to none."

"It's like a toaster, the ref's shirt pocket. Every time there's a tackle, up pops a yellow card. I'm talking metaphysically now, of course."

"I'd love to be a mole on the wall in the Liverpool dressing room at half-time. And not for the reasons that you're thinking of, Clive."

"The game has gone rather scrappy as both sides realise they could win this match or lose it or draw it even."

"I don't think there's anyone bigger or smaller than Maradona. You seen the pictures as well Clive. Like an acorn I tells ya, just like an acorn."

"I know what is around the corner. I just don't know where the corner is."

"You can't do better than go away from home and get a draw."

"...using his strength. And that is his strength, his strength. You could say that that's his strong point."

"The ref was vertically 15 yards away. He has a moustache."

"I came to Nantes two years ago and it's much the same today, except that it's totally different.

"Argentina are the second-best team in the world, and there's no higher praise than that."

"A tremendous strike which hit the defender full on the arm - and it nearly came off."
"The good news for Nigeria is that they're two-nil down very early in the game."

"That decision, for me, was almost certainly definitely wrong."

"I think Ron will be pulling him off at half time and no mistakin'."

"You'd think the Moroccans would have learnt their lesson by now. You can't win games without scoring goals."

"You'd think the Cameroonians would have learnt their lesson now. You can't get very far with such brutal tackles. It's just not cricket, you know."

"Louis Figo is different to David Beckham and vice versa"

"It was still moving when it hit the back of the net"

"Zero-sero's a big score sometimes"

"In some ways, cramp is worse than having a broken leg. But leukemia is worse still. Probably."

Cricket match comment:
Cook will declare with a lead of 350, we'll roll NZ for 300 and it'll all be worth it when I fail my exam tomorrow. (England v NZ May 2015)

Tim, Bristol

Quotes from Famous People

"In my many years I have come to a conclusion that one useless man is a shame, two is a law firm and three or more is a government."

John Adams

"If you don't read the newspaper you are uninformed, if you do read the newspaper you are misinformed."

Anon, but often attributed to Mark Twain.

"I contend that for a nation to try to tax itself into prosperity is like a man standing in a bucket and trying to lift himself up by the handle."

Winston Churchill

"A government which robs Peter to pay Paul can always depend on the support of Paul."

George Bernard Shaw

"Foreign aid might be defined as a transfer of money from poor people in rich countries to rich people in poor countries."

Attributed to various people including Douglas Casey, Classmate of Bill Clinton at Georgetown University

"Giving money and power to government is like giving whiskey and car keys to teenage boys."

P.J. O'Rourke, Civil Libertarian

"Government is the great fiction, through which everybody endeavours to live at the expense of everybody else."

Frederic Bastiat, French economist

"I don't make jokes. I just watch the government and report the facts."

Will Rogers

"In general, the art of government consists of taking as much money as possible from one part of the citizens to give to the other."

Voltaire

"Just because you do not take an interest in politics doesn't mean politics won't take an interest in you!"

Pericles

"No man's life, liberty, or property is safe while the legislature is in session."

Gideon Tucker (US lawyer and politician)

"Talk is cheap...except when government does it."

Anonymous, often attributed to Cullen Hightower

"The government is like a baby's alimentary canal, with a happy appetite at one end and no responsibility at the other."

Ronald Reagan

"The only difference between a tax man and a taxidermist is that the taxidermist leaves the skin."

Mark Twain

"What this country needs are more unemployed politicians."

Edward Langley, artist. Also attributed to Angela Davis,
political activist.

"A government big enough to give you everything you want, is strong enough to take everything you have."

Gerald Ford, address to 1974 address to Congress

"We hang the petty thieves and appoint the great ones to public office."

Aesop

"If you think health care is expensive now, wait until you see what it costs when it's free!"

P.J. O'Rourke

"It isn't pollution that's harming the environment. It's the impurities in our air and water that are doing it."

Attrib to Al Gore, Vice President & Dan Quayle
Believed to have been written by unknown humorists

"If we don't succeed, we run the risk of failure."

Attrib to George W.Bush

British Newspapers

Commenting on a complaint from a Mr. Arthur Purdey about a large gas bill, a spokesman for North West Gas said, "We agree it was rather high for the time of year. It's possible Mr. Purdey has been charged for the gas used up during the explosion that destroyed his house."

The Daily Telegraph

At the height of the gale, the harbour-master radioed a coast guard and asked him to estimate the wind speed. He replied that he was sorry, but he didn't have a gauge. However, if it was any help, the wind had just blown his Land Rover off the cliff.

Aberdeen Evening Express

Mrs. Irene Graham of Thorpe Avenue, Boscombe, delighted the audience with her reminiscence of the German prisoner of war who was sent each week to do her garden. He was repatriated at the end of 1945, she recalled: 'He'd always seemed a nice friendly chap, but when the crocuses came up in the middle of our lawn in February 1946, they spelt out 'Heil Hitler."

Bournemouth Evening Echo

source unknown

Police are being handicapped in a search for a stolen van, because they cannot issue a description. It's a Special Branch vehicle and they don't want the public to know what it looks like.

The Guardian

The editors were unable to verify these attributions

☺   ☺   ☺

Adverts Seen in Newspapers:

'Single male seeks double jointed supermodel who owns a brewery. Access to free concert tickets a plus.'

'Free to a good country home: 3/4 Rottweiler, 1/4 Shepherd, 3 years old, female, spayed, very intelligent, loves to eat live rabbits and kittens, loves to play ball with kids. Call after 5pm.'

Exam Howlers:

History:
In wartime children who lived in big cities had to be evaporated because it was safer in the country.

Sometimes in war they take prisners and keep them as ostriges until the war is over. Some prisners end up in consterpation camps.

Sir Walter Raleigh circumcised the world with a big clipper.

Maths:
The total is when you add up all the numbers and the remainder is an animal that pulls Santa on his slay.

If it is less than 90 degrees it is a cute angel.

I would like to be an accountant but you have to know a lot about moths.

The arts:
... and at the end of the show we all sang away in a manager.

In last year's Christmas concert Lindzi played the main prat. I played one of the smaller prats and I would like to have a bigger prat this year.

Science:

Helicopters are cleverer than planes. Not only can they fly through the air they can also hoover.

Geography:

In geography we learned that countries with sea all round them are islands and ones without sea are incontinents.

In Scandinavia, the Danish people come from Denmark, the Norwegians come from Norway and the Lapdancers come from Lapland.

Natural history:

Crabs and creatures like them or belong to a family of crushed asians.

Holidays:

The closet town to France is Dover. You can get to France on a train or you can go on a fairy.

... and if you think we forgot to spell check this section, you'd be wrong, it is what the children actually wrote.

☺   ☺   ☺

"Smoking kills. If you're killed, you've lost a very important part of your life."
Brooke Shields, during an interview to become spokesperson for federal anti-smoking campaign.

Military Advice

1. "Aim towards the enemy."
   (Instruction printed on U.S. Army rocket launcher.)

2. "When the pin is pulled, Mr. Grenade is not our friend."
   (U.S. Army training notice.)

3. "Cluster bombing from B-52s is very, very accurate. From 30,000 feet, every single bomb always hits the ground."
   (U.S. Air Force ammunition memo.)

4. "If you see a bomb disposal technician running, try to keep up with him."
   (U.S. Army ordnance manual.)

5. "It is generally inadvisable to eject directly over the area you just bombed."
   (U.S. Air Force flight training manual.)

The editors were unable to verify these quotes.

☺   ☺   ☺

"We have a firm commitment to NATO, we are a part of NATO. We have a firm commitment to Europe. We are a part of Europe."
George W. Bush

Give Way or Else

Transcript of a US naval ship with Canadian authorities off the coast of Newfoundland in October, 1995. This radio conversation was released by the Chief of Naval Operations on 10-10-95.

Americans: "Please divert your course 15 degrees to the North to avoid a collision."

Canadians: "Recommend you divert YOUR course 15 degrees to the South to avoid a collision."

Americans: "This is the captain of a US Navy ship. I say again, divert YOUR course."

Canadians: "No, I say again, you divert YOUR course."

Americans: "This is the aircraft carrier USS Abraham Lincoln, the second largest ship in the United States' Atlantic fleet. We are accompanied by three destroyers, three cruisers and numerous support vessels. I demand that you change your course 15 degrees north. That's one-five degrees north, or counter measures will be undertaken to ensure the safety of this ship."

Canadians: "This is a lighthouse. Your call."

For you to note all the less than intelligent
things you have heard.

4 When Work Gets You Down

If you've ever worked for a boss who reacts before getting the facts and thinking things through, you will love this....

A major steel company, feeling it was time for a shakeup, hired a new CEO. The new boss was determined to rid the company of all slackers.

On a tour of the facilities, the CEO noticed a guy leaning against a wall. The room was full of workers and he wanted to let them know that he meant business. He asked the guy, "How much money do you make a week?"

A little surprised, the young man looked at him and said, "I make $400 a week. Why?"

The CEO said, "Wait here." He walked back to his office, came back in two minutes, and handed the guy $1,600 in cash and said, "Here's four weeks' pay. Now GET OUT and don't come back."

Feeling pretty good about himself, the CEO looked around the room and asked, "Does anyone want to tell me what that goof-ball did here?"

From across the room a voice said, "He's the pizza delivery guy."

Hot Air Management

A man in a hot air balloon realised he was lost so he reduced altitude and spotted a woman below. He descended a little more and shouted: "Excuse me, can you help me. I promised a friend that I would meet him an hour ago, but I don't know where I am."

The woman replied:
"You are in a hot air balloon hovering approximately 30 feet above the ground. You are between 40 and 41 degrees North latitude and between 59 and 60 degrees west longitude"

"You must be an Engineer" said the balloonist. "Everything you told me is technical! It's correct, but I have no idea what to make of your information, and the fact is I am still lost. Frankly you have not been much help so far."

The woman below responded " You must be in management"

"I am" replied the balloonist "but how did you know?"

"Well", said the woman "You don't know where you are or where you are going. You have risen to where you are due to a large quantity of hot air.

☞ ☞ ☞

You made a promise which you have no idea how to keep, and you expect people beneath you to solve your problems. The fact is you are in exactly the same position you were in before we met, but now, somehow it's my fault."

☺   ☺   ☺

Whenever you are having a rough day, try this stress management technique recommended in the latest psychological journals. The funny thing is that it really does work and will make you smile...

1. Picture yourself lying on your belly on a warm rock that hangs out over a crystal clear stream.
2. Picture yourself with both your hands dangling in the cool running water.
3. Birds are sweetly singing in the cool mountain air.
4. No one knows your secret place.
5. You are in total seclusion from that hectic place called the world.
6. The soothing sound of a gentle waterfall fills the air with a cascade of serenity.
7. The water is so clear that you can easily make out the face of the person you are holding underwater.

There!! See? It really does work... You're smiling already.

The SAS, the Paras, the Police, & a Rabbit.

The SAS, the Parachute Regiment and the Police decide to go on a survival weekend together to see who comes out on top. After some basic exercises the trainer tells them that their next objective is to go down into the woods and catch a rabbit, returning with it ready to skin and cook.

Night falls.

First up - the SAS. They don the very latest night vision goggles, drop to the ground and crawl into the woods in formation. Absolute silence for five minutes, followed by the unmistakable muffled "phut-phut" of their trademark silenced "double-tap". They emerge with a large rabbit shot cleanly between the eyes.

"Excellent!" remarks the trainer.

Next up - the Paras. They finish their cans of lager, smear themselves with camouflage cream, fix bayonets and charge down into the woods, screaming at the top of their lungs. For the next hour the woods ring with the sound of rifle and machine-gun fire, hand grenades, mortar bombs and blood curdling war cries. Eventually they emerge, carrying the charred remains of a rabbit.

☞   ☞   ☞

"A bit messy, but you achieved the aim; well done." says the trainer.

Lastly, in go the police, walking slowly, hands behind backs whistling Dixon of Dock Green. For the next few hours, the silence is only broken by the occasional crackle of a walkie-talkie "Sierra Lima Whisky Tango Foxtrot One, suspect headed straight for you..." etc. After what seems an eternity, they emerge escorting a squirrel in handcuffs.

"What the hell do you think you are doing?" asks the incredulous trainer, "Take this squirrel back and get me a rabbit like I told you five hours ago!".

So back they go. Minutes pass. Minutes turn to hours, night drags on and turns to day. The next morning, the trainer and the other teams are awakened by the police, holding the handcuffed squirrel, now covered in bruises, one eye nearly shut.

"You cannot be serious!!" screamed the now highly irate trainer.

The police team leader nudges the squirrel, who squeaks:
"Alright, alright, I'm a rabbit!"

Hover Cats

An engineer was tasked with developing a futuristic, yet simple method of train travel.

When a cat is dropped, it always lands on its feet, and when toast is dropped, it always lands buttered side down. Therefore, if a slice of toast is strapped to a cat's back, buttered side up, and the animal is then dropped, the two opposing forces will cause it to hover, spinning inches above the ground. *If enough toast-laden felines were used, they could form the basis of a high-speed monorail system.*

Taking this further, in the buttered toast case, it's the butter that causes it to land buttered side down - it doesn't have to be toast, the theory works equally well with cheese crackers. So to save money you just miss out the toast – and butter the cats. Also, should there be an imbalance between the effects of cat and butter, there are other substances that have a stronger affinity for carpet.

Probability of carpet impact is determined by the following simple formula:

$$p = s * t(t)/tc$$

☞   ☞   ☞

where:

p is the probability of carpet impact,

s is the 'stain' value of the toast-covering substance - an indicator of the effectiveness of the toast topping in permanently staining the carpet. Chicken tikka masala, for example, has a very high s value, while the s value of water is zero.

tc and t(t) indicate the tone of the carpet and topping - the value of p being strongly related to the relationship between the colour of the carpet and topping, as even chicken tikka masala won't cause a permanent and obvious stain if the carpet is the same colour.

So it is obvious that the probability of carpet impact is maximised if you use chicken tikka masala and a white carpet - in fact this combination gives a p value of one, which is the same as the probability of a cat landing on its feet.

Therefore a cat with chicken tikka masala on its back will be certain to hover in mid air, while there could be problems with buttered toast as the toast may fall off the cat, causing a terrible monorail crash resulting in politicians saying it wouldn't have happened if their party was in power as there would have been more investment in cat-toast adhesion research.

Therefore it is in the interests not only of public safety but also public sanity if the buttered toast on cats idea is scrapped, to be replaced by a monorail powered by cats smeared with chicken tikka masala floating above a rail made from white shag pile carpet.

☺   ☺   ☺

Caller: "Can you give me the telephone number for Jack?"

Operator: "I'm sorry, sir, I don't understand who you are talking about."

Caller: "On page 1, section 5, of the user guide it clearly states that I need to unplug the fax machine from the AC wall socket and telephone jack before cleaning. Now, can you give me the number for Jack?"

☺   ☺   ☺

Caller: "Could you give me the number of the knitwear company in Woven."

Operator: (pause) "Woven? Are you sure?"

Caller: "Yes. That's what it says on the label: Woven in Scotland."

Job Application

Murphy applied for a fermentation operator post at a famous Irish firm based in Dublin. A Pole applied for the same job and since both applicants had similar qualifications, they were asked to take a test by the Manager.

When the results were in, both men had scored 19 out of 20. The manager went to Murphy and said, "Thank you for coming to the interview, but we've decided to give the Pole the job."

Murphy: "And why would you be doing that? We both got 19 questions correct. This being Ireland and me being Irish surely I should get the job."

Manager: "We have made our decision not on the correct answers, but on the question you got wrong."

Murphy: "And just how would one incorrect answer be better than another?"

Manager: "Simple. On question number 7 the Pole wrote down, 'I don't know.' You put down, 'Neither do I'."

Microsoft vs GM

At a recent computer expo (COMDEX), Bill Gates reportedly compared the computer industry with the auto industry and stated: "If GM had kept up with technology like the computer industry has, we would all be driving $25 cars that got 1,000 miles to the gallon."

In response to Bill's comments, General Motors issued a press release stating: If GM had developed technology like Microsoft, we would all be driving cars with the following characteristics:

1. For no reason whatsoever, your car would crash........Twice a day.

2. Every time they repainted the lines in the road, you would have to buy a new car.

3. Occasionally your car would die on the freeway for no reason. You would have to pull to the side of the road, close all of the windows, shut off the car, restart it, and reopen the windows before you could continue. For some reason you would simply accept this.

4. Occasionally, executing a maneuver such as a left turn would cause your car to shut down and

☞ ☞ ☞

refuse to restart, in which case you would have to reinstall the engine.

5. Macintosh would make a car that was powered by the sun, was reliable, five times as fast and twice as easy to drive - but would run on only five percent of the roads.

6 The oil, water temperature, and alternator warning lights would all be replaced by a single 'This Car Has Performed An Illegal Operation' warning light.

7. The airbag system would ask 'Are you sure?' before deploying.

8. Occasionally, for no reason whatsoever, your car would lock you out and refuse to let you in until you simultaneously lifted the door handle, turned the key and grabbed hold of the radio antenna.

9. Every time a new car was introduced car buyers would have to learn how to drive all over again because none of the controls would operate in the same manner as the old car.

10. You'd have to press the 'Start' button to turn the engine off.

PS - I'd like to add that when all else fails, you could call 'customer service' in some foreign country and be instructed in some foreign language how to fix your car yourself!!!!

Whilst this makes a fun story, it is not true. According to Snopes, the story can be traced back to a much simpler version in 1997. Since then it has grown arms and legs (or whatever the equivalent is for a computer)

☺   ☺   ☺

Credit Card Security?

I was signing the receipt for my credit card purchase when the clerk noticed I had never signed my name on the back of the credit card.

She informed me that she could not complete the transaction unless the card was signed.

When I asked why, she explained that it was necessary to compare the signature I had just signed on the receipt with the credit card signature. So I signed the credit card in front of her. She carefully compared the signature to the one I had just signed on the receipt.

As luck would have it, they matched!

A Wish List Come True

A sales rep, an administration clerk, and their manager are walking to lunch together when they find an antique oil lamp. They decide to rub it and a genie comes out (well, it would, wouldn't it).

"I'll give each of you one wish." says the genie

"Me first! Me first!" pleads the admin clerk. "I want to be in the Bahamas, driving a speedboat, without a care in the world." Puff! She is gone.

"Me next! Me next!" begs the sales rep excitedly. "I want to be in Hawaii , relaxing on the beach with my personal masseure, an endless supply of Pina Coladas and the love of my life." Puff! He's gone.

The genie turns to the manager saying: "OK, you're turn." The manager says: "I want those two back in the office after lunch."

Moral of the story:
Always let your boss have the first say.

☺   ☺   ☺

The trouble with doing something right the first time is that nobody appreciates how difficult it was.

Monkey Games & Company Policy

Start with a cage containing five monkeys. Inside the cage, hang banana on a string and place a set of stairs under it. Before long, a monkey will go to the stairs and start to climb towards the banana. As soon as he touches the stairs, spray all of the other monkeys with cold water.

After a while, another monkey makes an attempt with the same result - all the other monkeys are sprayed with cold water. Pretty soon, when another monkey tries to climb the stairs, the other monkeys will try to prevent it.

Now, put away the cold water. Remove one monkey from the cage and replace it with a new one. The new monkey sees the banana and wants to climb the stairs. To his surprise and horror, all of the other monkeys attack him. After another attempt and attack, he knows that if he tries to climb the stairs, he will be assaulted.

Next, remove another of the original five monkeys and replace it with a new one. The newcomer goes to the stairs and is attacked. The previous newcomer takes part in the punishment with enthusiasm!

Likewise, replace a third original monkey with a new one, then a fourth, then the fifth. Every time the newest monkey takes to the stairs, he is attacked.

Most of the monkeys that are beating him have no idea why they were not permitted to climb the stairs or why they are participating in the beating of the newest monkey.

After replacing all the original monkeys, none of the remaining monkeys have ever been sprayed with cold water. Nevertheless, no monkey ever again approaches the stairs to try for the banana. Why not? - Because as far as they know that's the way it's always been done around here.

And that is how company policy begins.

*An experiment carried out by Stephenson in 1966 is sometimes quoted as supporting this story, but in fact it does not. However, **we** believe the experiment does, in fact, explain company policy development!*

☺   ☺   ☺

A manager comes out of his office to see his new clerk talking to an envelope. Intrigued, he asks the clerk "Why are you talking to the envelope?"
"I'm sending a voicemail" comes the reply.

Origins of Engineering Specs. and Government Decisions.

Ever wonder where engineering specifications come from? The US standard railroad gauge (distance between the rails) is 4 feet 8.5 inches, an exceedingly odd number.

Why was that gauge used? Because that's the way they built them in England, and the English built the first US railroads.

Why did the English build them like that? Because the first rail lines were built by the people who built the pre-railroad tramways, and that is the gauge they used.

Why did they use that particular gauge then? Because the people who built the tramways used the same jigs and tools that they used for building wagons, which used the same wheel spacing.

Why did the wagons have that particular odd wheel spacing? Well, if they tried to use any other spacing, the wagon wheels would break on the old, long distance roads in England, because that's the spacing of the wheel ruts in the granite sets. So, who built those old rutted roads? Imperial Rome built the first long distance roads in Europe (and England) for their legions. The roads have been

☞   ☞   ☞

used ever since. And the ruts in the roads? Roman war chariots formed the initial ruts, which everyone else had to match for fear of destroying their wagon wheels. Since the chariots were made for (or by) Imperial Rome, they all had the same wheel spacing. The United States standard railroad gauge of 4 feet, 8.5 inches is derived from the specification for an Imperial Roman war chariot. Specifications and Bureaucracies live forever. The Imperial Roman war chariots were made just wide enough to accommodate the back ends of two war-horses.

Now let's cut to the present. The Space Shuttle, sitting on its launch pad, has two booster rockets attached to the sides of the main fuel tank. These are solid rocket boosters, or SRBs. A company builds SRBs at its factory in Utah. The engineers who designed the SRBs wanted to make them a bit fatter, but the SRBs had to be shipped by train from the factory to the launch site. The railroad line from the factory has to run through a tunnel in the mountains. The SRBs had to fit through that tunnel, which is slightly wider than the railroad track, and the railroad track is about as wide as two horses' behinds. So.... a major design feature of what is arguably the world's most advanced transportation system was determined two thousand years ago by a horse's rear end.

☞ ☞ ☞

Which is pretty much how most government decisions are made.

This article was written by Marty Riske, Fargo and tracked down to the North Dakota Mensa site. Thanks Marty.

Editors

☺   ☺   ☺

Quotes from Employee Performance Evaluations

"Works well only when under constant supervision and cornered like a rat in a trap.

"His men would follow him anywhere, but only out of morbid curiosity."

"He's so dense, light bends around him."

"This employee is really not so much of a 'has-been', but more of a definite 'won't be.'"

"Since my last report, he has reached rock bottom and has started to dig."

"When she opens her mouth, it seems that it is to change whichever foot was previously in there."

Evaluating Departments

A managing director wanted to evaluate the initiative of his employees, so at a weekly meeting he presented the Finance, Sales and IT department with a task. He said "Next week I want each of you to give a talk using these as the central prop" and handed each department two ball bearings.

The following week the departments met and gave their talks.

The Finance department began: "We attached some thread to each ball and hung them both in a frame made out of pencils sellotaped together thus creating a simple Newton's Cradle. This helps to show the principals of the conservation of energy."

The Sales department followed with: "We stretched a split balloon over the top of this waste paper basket. We then placed one ball bearing in the middle and rolled the second ball around the first one. This helps explain how mass distorts space, showing the effects of gravity in two dimensions using the second ball as an orbiting object."

Then came the IT departments turn:
"We broke one and lost the other."

Australian Bricklayer Report

This is a bricklayer's accident report, which is reported to have printed in the newsletter of the Australian equivalent of the Workers' Compensation Board.

Dear Sir,

I am writing in response to your request for additional information in Block 3 of the accident report form. I put "poor planning" as the cause of my accident. You asked for a fuller explanation and I trust the following details will be sufficient.

I am a bricklayer by trade. On the day of the accident, I was working alone on the roof of a new six-story building. When I completed my work, I found that I had some bricks left over which, when weighed later were found to weigh slightly in excess of 500lbs. Rather than carry the bricks down by hand, I decided to lower them in a barrel by using a pulley, which was attached to the side of the building on the sixth floor.

Securing the rope at ground level I went up on to the roof, and swung the barrel out and loaded the bricks into it. Then I went down and untied the rope, holding it tightly to ensure a slow descent of the bricks.

☞ ☞ ☞

You will note in Block 11 of the accident report form that I weigh 135lbs. Due to my surprise at being jerked off the ground so suddenly, I lost my presence of mind and forgot to let go of the rope. Needless to say, I proceeded at a rapid rate up the side of the building. In the vicinity of the third floor, I met the barrel, which was now proceeding downward at an equally impressive speed. This explained the fractured skull, minor abrasions and the broken collar bone, as listed in section 3 of the accident report form.

Slowed only slightly, I continued my rapid ascent, not stopping until the fingers of my right hand were two knuckles deep into the pulley.

Fortunately by this time I had regained my presence of mind and was able to hold tightly to the rope, in spite of beginning to experience pain. At approximately the same time, however, the barrel of bricks hit the ground and the bottom fell out of the barrel. Now devoid of the weight of the bricks, that barrel weighed approximately 50 lbs. I refer you again to my weight.

As you can imagine, I began a rapid descent down the side of the building. In the vicinity of the third floor, I met the barrel coming up. This accounts for the two fractured ankles, broken tooth and several lacerations of my legs and lower body.

☞ ☞ ☞

Here my luck began to change slightly. The encounter with the barrel seemed to slow me enough to lessen my injuries when I fell into the pile of bricks and fortunately only three vertebrae were cracked.

I am sorry to report, however, as I lay there on the pile of bricks, in pain and unable to move, I again lost my composure and presence of mind and let go of the rope and I lay there watching the empty barrel begin its journey back down onto me. This explains the two broken legs.

I hope this answers your inquiry.

A. Bricklayer

☺   ☺   ☺

Do You Work for Directory Enquiries?

Caller: "I'd like the number of the Argoed Fish Bar in Cardiff please."
Operator: "I'm sorry, there's no listing. Is the spelling correct?"
Caller: "Well, it used to be called the Bargoed Fish Bar but the 'B' fell off the sign".

A Tie, Water and... well, a Few Other Things

A man who had crash landed his plane was plodding through the desert desperate for water when he saw something far off in the distance. Hoping there might be water there, he staggered toward the object, only to find a little old woman at a small stand selling neckties.

The man asked, "Do you have water?" The old woman replied, "I have no water. Would you like to buy a tie? They are only $5."

"The man shouted, "Stupid woman!" and in his distress proceed to insult her and her ancestors. "I don't need an overpriced tie. I need water!"

"OK," said the old woman, "it does not matter that you don't want to buy a tie and that you hate me. I will show you that I am bigger than that. If you continue over that hill to the east for about two miles, you will find a lovely restaurant. It has all the water you need. Safe journey."

Muttering, the man staggered away over the hill.

Several hours later he staggered back.
"Your brother won't let me in without a tie."

Administration

The U.S. Army Laboratory at Natick, Ma. has recently announced the discovery of the heaviest element yet known to science. This new element has been tentatively named "Administratium".

Administratium has 1 neutron, 12 assistant neutrons, 75 deputy neutrons, and 111 assistant deputy neutrons, giving it an atomic mass of 312. These 312 particles are held together by a force called morons, which are surrounded by vast quantities of lepton-like particles called peons.

Since Administratium has no electrons, it is inert. However, it can be detected as it impedes every reaction with which it comes into contact. A minute amount of Administratium causes one reaction to take over four days to complete when it would normally take less than a second.

Administratium has a normal half-life of three years; it does not decay but instead undergoes a reorganization, in which a portion of the assistant neutrons and deputy neutrons and assistant deputy neutrons exchange places. In fact, Administratium's mass will actually increase over time, since each reorganization causes some morons to become neutrons forming isodopes.

☞ ☞ ☞

This characteristic of moron-promotion leads some scientists to speculate that Administratium is formed whenever morons reach a certain quantity in concentration. This hypothetical quantity is referred to as "Critical Morass."

You will know it when you see it.

☺   ☺   ☺

Tech Support: "I need you to right-click on the Open Desktop."
Customer: "OK."
Tech Support: "Did you get a pop-up menu?."
Customer: "No".
Tech Support: "OK. right-click again. Do you see a pop-up menu?"
Customer: "No."
Tech Support: "OK, sir. Can you tell me what you have done up until this point?."
Customer: "Sure. You told me to write 'click' and I wrote 'click'".

More Quotes From Employee Performance Evaluations

"This young lady has delusions of adequacy."

"He sets low personal standards and then consistently fails to achieve them."

How Large Corporations REALLY Work

Today's reading is from the Book of Project Management & Corporate Life, Chapter 1

1 In the beginning was the Plan.
2 And then came the Assumptions.
3 And the Assumptions were without form.
4 And the Plan was without Substance.
5 And darkness was upon the face of the Workers.
6 And the Workers spoke among themselves saying, "It is a crock of s..t and it stinks."
7 And the Workers went unto their Supervisors and said, "It is a crock of dung and we cannot live with the smell."
8 And the Supervisors went unto their Managers saying, "It is a container of organic waste, and it is very strong, such that none may abide by it."
9 And the Managers went unto their Directors, saying, "It is a vessel of fertilizer, and none may abide its strength."
10 And the Directors spoke among themselves, saying to one another, "It contains that which aids plant growth, and it is very strong."
11 And the directors went to the Vice Presidents saying unto them: "It promotes growth and it is very powerful"
12 And the Vice Presidents went to the President saying unto him: "It has very powerful effects"

☞ ☞ ☞

13 And the President looked upon the Plan and saw that it was good.

14 And the Plan became Policy.

15 And that is how s .. t happens.

☺   ☺   ☺

Cannibals at Work

A big corporation recently hired several cannibals. "You are all part of our team now", said the HR rep during the welcoming briefing. "You get all the usual benefits and you can go to the cafeteria for something to eat, but please don't eat any of the other employees." The cannibals promised they would not.

Four weeks later their boss remarked, "You're all working very hard, and I'm satisfied with you. However, one of our secretaries has disappeared. Do any of you know what happened to her?" The cannibals all shook their heads... no.

After the boss had left, the leader of the cannibals said to the others, "Which one of you idiots ate the secretary?" A hand raised hesitantly, to which the leader of the cannibals continued: "You fool!! For four weeks we've been eating Managers and no one noticed anything, but noooooo, you had to go and eat someone important!"

Recruitment Process in the CIA

The CIA had an opening for an assassin. After all of the background checks, interviews, and testing were done there were three finalists... two men and a woman.

For the final test, the CIA agents took one of the men to a large metal door and handed him a gun. "We must know that you will follow your instructions, no matter what the circumstances. Inside of this room, you will find your wife sitting in a chair. Kill her!!!"

The man said, "You can't be serious. I could never shoot my wife."

The agent said, "Then you're not the right man for this job."

The second man was given the same instructions. He took the gun and went into the room. All was quiet for about five minutes. Then the man came out with tears in his eyes. "I tried, but I can't kill my wife."

The agent said, "You don't have what it takes. Take your wife and go home."

☞ ☞ ☞

Finally, it was the woman's turn. She was given the same instructions: to kill her husband. She took the gun and went into the room. Shots were heard, one shot after another. They heard screaming, crashing, banging on the walls. After a few minutes, all was quiet. The door opened slowly and there stood the woman. She wiped the sweat from her brow, and said: "This gun is loaded with blanks. I had to beat him to death with the chair."

☺ ☺ ☺

Automobile Motoring Services

Caller: "Does your European Breakdown Policy cover me when I am travelling in Australia ?"

Operator: "Doesn't the product name give you a clue?"

☺ ☺ ☺

Driving in France

UK caller enquiring about legal requirements while travelling in France: "If I register my car in France, do I have to change the steering wheel to the other side of the car?"

For All You Medics

Supposedly real experiences as told by medics...

Dr. Susan Steinberg, Manitoba, Canada: I was performing a complete physical, including the visual acuity test. I placed the patient twenty feet from the chart and began, "Cover you right eye with your hand." He read the 20/20 line perfectly. "Now your left." Again, a flawless read. "Now both," I requested. There was silence. He couldn't even read the large E on the top line. I turned and discovered that he had done exactly what I had asked: he was standing there with both his eyes covered.

Dr. Matthew Theodropolous, Worcester MA: During a patient's two week follow-up appointment with his cardiologist, he informed me that he was having trouble with one of his medications. "Which one?" I asked. "The patch. The nurse told me to put on a new one every six hours and now I'm running out of places to put it!" I had him quickly undress and discovered what I hoped I wouldn't see... Yes, the man had over fifty patches on his body! Now the instructions include removal of the old patch before applying a new one.

We have been unable to validate these stories - Editors

 ☺ ☺ ☺

Virus Warning

This virus warning is genuine.

There is a new virus going around called Worm-Overload-Recreational-Killer (WORK) If you receive any sort of WORK at all, whether via email, internet or simply handed to you by a colleague...DO NOT OPEN IT.

WORK has been circulating around our building for months and those who have been tempted to open WORK or even look at WORK have found that their social life is deleted and their brain ceases to function properly.

If you receive WORK in paper-document form, simply lift the document and drag it to your in-office neutraliser, usually known as the WPB (Waste Paper Bin).

If you WORK via email then to purge the virus, send an email to your boss with the words "I've had enough of slaving for you day in, day out. I'm off to the pub." The WORK should automatically be forgotten by your brain. Put your jacket on and take two good friends to the nearest PUB (Public Un-virusing Bureau).

☞ ☞ ☞

Purchase the antidote known as Work-Isolator-Neutralizer-Extractor (WINE). The quickest acting WINE type is called Swift-Hitting-Infiltrator-Remover-All-Zones (SHIRAZ) but this is only available for those who can afford it. The next best equivalent is Cheapest-Available-System-Killer (CASK). Take the antidote repeatedly until WORK has been completely eliminated from your system.

☺   ☺   ☺

More Quotes from Employee Performance Evaluations

"This employee is depriving a village somewhere of an idiot."

"Not the sharpest knife in the drawer."

"Got into the gene pool while the lifeguard wasn't watching."

"A room temperature IQ."

"This employee should go far...and the sooner he starts, the better."

"A gross ignoramus - 144 times worse than an ordinary ignoramus."

For all of You in the Legal Profession:
Guilty as Charged.... or Not?

At the 1994 annual awards dinner given for Forensic Science, AAFS President Dr Don Harper Mills astounded his audience with the legal complications of a bizarre death. Here is the story as reported by Kurt Westervelt in the Associated Press

On March 23, 1994 the medical examiner viewed the body of Ronald Opus and concluded that he died from a shotgun wound to the head.

Mr. Opus had jumped from the top of a ten-story building intending to commit suicide. He left a note to the effect indicating his despondency.

As he fell past the ninth floor his life was interrupted by a shotgun blast passing through a window, which killed him instantly. Neither the shooter nor the deceased was aware that a safety net had been installed just below the eighth floor level to protect some building workers and that Ronald Opus would not have been able to complete his suicide the way he had planned.

"Ordinarily," Dr Mills continued, "A person who sets out to commit suicide and ultimately succeeds, even though the mechanism might not be what he intended, is still defined as committing suicide."

☞ ☞ ☞

121

That Mr. Opus was shot on the way to certain death, but probably would not have been successful because of the safety net, caused the medical examiner to feel that he had a homicide on his hands.

The room on the ninth floor, where the shotgun blast emanated, was occupied by an elderly man and his wife. They were arguing vigorously and he was threatening her with a shotgun. The man was so upset that when he pulled the trigger he completely missed his wife and the pellets went through the window striking Mr. Opus.

When one intends to kill subject "A" but kills subject "B" in the attempt, one is guilty of the murder of subject "B."

When confronted with the murder charge the old man and his wife were both adamant and both said that they thought the shotgun was unloaded. The old man said it was a long-standing habit to threaten his wife with the unloaded shotgun. He had no intention to murder her. Therefore the killing of Mr. Opus appeared to be an accident; that is, if the gun had been accidentally loaded.

The continuing investigation turned up a witness who saw the old couple's son loading the shotgun about six weeks prior to the fatal accident.

☞ ☞ ☞

It transpired that the old lady had cut off her son's financial support and the son, knowing the propensity of his father to use the shotgun threateningly, loaded the gun with the expectation that his father would shoot his mother.

Since the loader of the gun was aware of this, he was guilty of the murder even though he didn't actually pull the trigger. The case now becomes one of murder on the part of the son for the death of Ronald Opus.

Now comes the exquisite twist. Further investigation revealed that the son was, in fact, Ronald Opus. He had become increasingly despondent over the failure of his attempt to engineer his mother's murder. This led him to jump off the ten story building on March 23rd, only to be killed by a shotgun blast passing through the ninth story window. The son had actually murdered himself so the medical examiner closed the case as a suicide.

A great story (could make a great film?) but our research suggests that it is not true.

☺   ☺   ☺

Don't take life too seriously; no one gets out alive.

Write here all the things you love and hate
about your job

5 Heart-warming Stories to Help You Get the Most Out of Life

If a dog was the teacher you would learn stuff like:

- When a loved ones come home, always run to greet them.
- Allow the experience of fresh air and the wind in your face to be pure ecstasy.
- Let others know when they have invaded your territory.
- Run, romp, and play daily.
- Thrive on attention and let people touch you.
- Avoid biting when a simple growl will do.
- When you're happy, dance around and wag your entire body.
- Delight in the simple joy of a long walk.
- Eat with gusto and enthusiasm. Stop when you have had enough.
- Be loyal.
- Never pretend to be something you are not.
- If what you want lies buried, dig until you find it.
- When someone is having a bad day, be silent, sit close by and nuzzle them gently.

Stone

Two friends were walking through the desert. During some point of the journey they had an argument and one friend slapped the other in the face. The one who got slapped was hurt but without saying anything wrote in the sand:

Today my best friend slapped me in the face

They kept on walking until they found an oasis where they decided to take a swim. The one who had been slapped got stuck in the mire and started drowning but the friend saved him.

After he recovered from the near drowning he wrote on a stone:

Today my best friend saved my life

The friend who had slapped and saved his best friend ask him: "After I hurt you, you wrote in the sand and now you write on a stone, why?"

The friend replied: "When someone hurts us we should write it down in sand where the winds of forgiveness can erase it away. But when someone does something good for us we should engrave it in stone where no wind can ever erase it."

☞ ☞ ☞

Learn to write your hurts in the sand and to carve your benefits in stone.

They say it takes a minute to find a special person, an hour to appreciate them, day to love them, and an entire life to forget them.

Do not value the things you have in your life but value who you have known in your life.

Be kinder than necessary, for everyone you meet is fighting some kind of battle.

☺   ☺   ☺

How to Live Your Life

Give people more than they expect and do it cheerfully.

Marry a man/woman you love to talk to. As you get older, their conversational skills will be as important as any other.

Don't believe all you hear, spend all you have or sleep all you want.

When someone asks you a question you don't want to answer, smile and ask: "Why do you want to know?"

Rich & Poor

One day the father of a very wealthy American family took his son on a trip to the countryside with the express purpose of showing him how poor people live. They spent a couple of days and nights on the farm of what would be considered to be a very poor family.

On the return from their trip the father asked the son: "How was the trip?"
"It was great Dad" replied the son.

"Did you see how poor people live?" asked the father"
"Oh yeah!" Replied the son.

"So tell me, what did you learn from the trip?"
The son replied:
"I saw that we have one dog and they had four.
We have a pool that reaches to the middle of our garden and they have a creek that has no end.
We have imported lanterns in our garden and they have stars at night.
Our patio reaches to the front yard they have the whole horizon.
We have a small plot to live on they have fields that stretch beyond sight.
We have servants that serve us but they serve others.

☞   ☞   ☞

We buy our food, they grow theirs.
We have walls around our property to protect us, they have friends to protect them."

The boy's father was speechless and the son added: "Thank you Dad for showing me how poor we are."

Isn't perspective a wonderful thing. It makes you wonder what would happen if we all gave thanks for what we have instead of worrying about what we don't have.

Appreciate the simple things you have, especially your friends.

☺   ☺   ☺

Many people will walk in and out of your life. But only true friends will leave footprints in your heart.

To handle yourself, use your head; to handle others, use your heart.

Anger is only one letter short of danger.

A true friend is someone who reaches for your hand and touches your heart.

Yesterday is history - Tomorrow is a mystery.

The Professor

A philosophy professor stood before his class and had some items in front of him. When class began, wordlessly he picked up a large empty bucket and proceeded to fill it with rocks of about 2" diameter right to the top. He then asked the students if the bucket was full. They agreed that it was.

So the professor then picked up a box of pebbles and poured them in to the bucket. He shook the bucket lightly. The pebbles, of course, rolled into the open areas between the rocks. The students laughed. He asked his students again if the bucket was full. They agreed that yes, it was.

The professor then picked up a box of sand and poured it into the bucket. Of course, the sand filled up the remaining spaces.

"Now," said the professor, "I want you to recognize that this is your life. The rocks are the important things - your family, your partner, your health, your children - anything that is so important to you that if it were lost, you would be nearly destroyed. The pebbles are the other things in life that matter, but on smaller scale. The pebbles represent things like your job, your house, your car. The sand is everything else. The small stuff.

☞ ☞ ☞

If you put the sand or the pebbles into the bucket first, there is no room for the rocks. The same goes for your life. If you spend all your energy and time on the small stuff, material things, you will never have room for the things that are truly most important. Pay attention to the things that are critical in your life. Play with your children. Take your partner out dancing. There will always be time to go to work, clean the house, give a dinner party and fix the drain pipe.

Take care of the rocks first-the things that really matter. Set your priorities. The rest is just pebbles and sand.

Special people

Do not value the things you have in your life,
but value who you have known in your life!

When you say, 'I'm sorry,' look the person in the eye.

Don't let a little dispute injure a great friendship.

What Can We Learn From a Donkey?

Part 1:
One day a farmer's donkey fell down into a well. The animal cried piteously for hours as the farmer tried to figure out what to do. Finally, he decided that the animal was old, and the well needed to be covered up anyway, it just wasn't worth it to retrieve the donkey.

He invited all his neighbours to come over and help him. They all grabbed shovels and began to shovel dirt into the well. At first, the donkey realized what was happening and cried horribly. Then, to everyone's amazement he quietened down.

A few shovel loads later, the farmer finally looked down the well. He was astonished at what he saw. With each shovel of dirt that hit his back, the donkey was doing something amazing. He would shake it off and take a step up.

As the farmer's neighbours continued to shovel dirt on top of the animal, he would shake it off and take a step up. Pretty soon, everyone was amazed as the donkey stepped up over the edge of the well and happily trotted off!

Life is going to shovel dirt on you, all kinds of dirt.

☞ ☞ ☞

The trick to getting out of the well is to shake it off and take a step up. Each of our troubles is a steppingstone. We can get out of the deepest wells just by not stopping by never giving up! Shake it off and take a step up.

Part 2:
The donkey later came back. He was so furious at what the farmer had tried to do to him that he bit, chased and kicked the farmer until, exhausted, the donkey wandered off and disappeared forever.

The gashes and cuts the farmer got from the irate donkey got infected, and the farmer eventually died in agony from septic shock.

The moral of the story is: when you do something wrong, it always comes back to bite you.

☺　☺　☺

Friends

Friends, you and me ....
You brought another friend and then there were three.
We started our group .... our circle of friends.
There is no beginning and there is no end.

I'll Be Happy When...

We convince ourselves that life will be better after we get married, have a baby, then another.

Then we are frustrated that the kids aren't old enough and we'll be more content when they are.

After that, we're frustrated that we have teenagers to deal with. We will certainly be happy when they are out of that stage.

We tell ourselves that our life will be complete when our spouse gets his or her act together, when we get a better car, when we are able to go on a nice vacation or when we retire.

The truth is that there is no better time to be happy than right now. If not now, when? Your life will always be full of challenges.

It is best to admit this to yourself and to decide to be happy anyway. Happiness is the way. So, treasure every moment that you have and treasure it more because you shared it with someone special, special enough to spend your time with ... and remember that time waits for no one.

☞ ☞ ☞

So, stop waiting ...
Until your car or home is paid off.
Until you get a new car or home.
Until your kids leave the house.
Until you go back to school.
Until you finish school.
Until you lose 10 lbs.
Until you gain 10 lbs.
Until you get married.
Until you get a divorce.
Until you have kids.
Until you retire.
Until summer.
Until spring.
Until winter.
Until fall.
Until you die.

There is no better time than right now to be happy. Happiness is a journey, not a destination.

So work like you don't need money, love like you've never been hurt, and dance like no one's watching.

Never laugh at anyone's dreams.
People who don't have dreams don't have much.

Instructions for Life

The Dalai Lama's 18 rules for living...

1. Take into account that great love and great achievements involve great risk.
2. When you lose, don't lose the lesson.
3. Follow the 3Rs:
   - respect for self
   - respect for others
   - responsibility for your actions.
4. Remember that not getting what you want is sometimes a wonderful stroke of luck.
5. Learn the rules so that you will know how to break them properly.
6. Don't let a little dispute ruin a great relationship.
7. When you realise you have made a mistake take immediate steps to correct it.
8. Spend time alone every day.
9. Open your arms to change but do not let go of your values.
10. Remember that silence is sometimes the best answer.
11. Live a good honourable life. Then when you get older you will be able to enjoy it a second time.
12. A loving atmosphere in your home is the foundation for your life.

☞ ☞ ☞

13. In disagreements with loved ones, deal only with the current situation - don't bring up the past.
14. Share your knowledge: it is a way to achieve immortality.
15. Be gentle with the Earth, it's where we live.
16. Once a year go someplace you've never been before.
17. Remember that the best relationship is one in which your love for each other exceeds your need for each other.
18. Judge your success by what you had to give up in order to achieve it.

☺   ☺   ☺

If someone betrays you once, it is his fault; if he betrays you twice, it is your fault.

Great minds discuss ideas,
Average minds discuss events,
Small minds discuss people.

Learn from the mistakes of others. You can't live long enough to make them all yourself.

In disagreements, fight fairly. No name calling.

Don't judge people by their relatives.

The Dash (-)

I read of a man who stood to speak
At the funeral of a friend.
He referred to the dates on her tombstone,
From the beginning ... to the end.

He noted that first came her date of birth
And spoke that date with tears,
But he said what mattered most of all
Was the dash between those years.

(1924 - 2015)

For that dash represents all the time
That she spent alive on earth.
And now only those who loved her,
Know what that little line is worth.

For it matters not, how much we own;
The cars... the house... the cash.
What matters is how we live and love
And how we spend our dash.

So think about this long and hard...
Are there things you'd like to change?
For you never know how much time is left,
That can still be rearranged.

☞ ☞ ☞

If we could just slow down enough
To consider what's true and real,
And always try to understand
The way other people feel.

And be less quick to anger,
And show appreciation more
And love the people in our lives
Like we've never loved before.

If we treat each other with respect,
And more often wear a smile.
Remembering that this special dash
Might only last a little while.

So, when your eulogy's being read
With your life's actions to rehash.
Would you be proud of the things they say
About how you spent your dash?

Anon.

☺   ☺   ☺

Love deeply and passionately. You might get hurt,
but it's the only way to live life completely.

Smile when picking up the phone. The caller will
hear it in your voice.

I've learned that it takes years to build up trust but
only takes suspicion, not proof, to destroy it.

Money

It can buy a house ..... but not a home
It can buy a clock ..... but not time
It can buy a position ..... but not respect
It can buy a bed ..... but not peaceful sleep
It can buy a book ..... but not knowledge
It can buy medicine ..... but not health
It can buy blood ..... but not life

So you see, money isn't everything.
And it often causes pain and suffering.
I tell you this because I am your friend and I want
to take away your suffering

So, send me all your money and I will suffer for
you.
(cash only, please)

☺   ☺   ☺

He, who loses money, loses much;
He, who loses a friend, loses much more;
He, who loses faith, loses all.

Robert E. Lee

That money talks it is no lie,
I heard it once, it said: "bye bye"

Richard Armour

How to Achieve Inner Peace

By following the simple advice I read in an article, I have finally found inner peace....

It read: "The way to achieve inner peace is to finish all the things you've started."

I looked around to see all the things that I started but hadn't finished. So, today I have finished:
- one bottle of vodka,
- a bottle of red wine,
- a bottle of Jack Daniel's,
- my Prozac,
- a small box of chocolates and
- a shot of tequila.

You have no idea how good I feel.

The best way to succeed in life is to act on the advice you give to others.

The mind is like a parachute -
It works best when it is open!

Every obstacle presents an opportunity to improve our condition.

If you were your best friend what advice would you give yourself?

6 Weird Thoughts, Puzzles and Facts to Feed your Brain

Re-arranging the Letters

The words below can be re-arranged to give a word or phrase related to it.

For example:

Presbyterian becomes Best in prayer

Try these - the answers are on the next page.

Astronomer	_____
Desperation	_____
The eyes	_____
George Bush	_____
The Morse Code	_____
Dormitory	_____
Slot machines	_____
Animosity	_____
Election results	_____
Snooze alarms	_____
A decimal point	_____
The Earthquakes	_____
Eleven plus two	_____
Mother-in-law	_____

☞ ☞ ☞

Re-arranging the Letters: answers:

Astronomer	moon starer
Desperation	a rope ends it
The eyes	they see
George Bush	he barks gore
The Morse code	here come dots
Dormitory	dirty room
Slot machines	cash lost in me
Animosity	is no amity
Election results	lies let's recount
Snooze alarms	alas! No more z's
A decimal point	I'm a dot in place
The earthquakes	that queer shake
Eleven plus two	twelve plus one
Mother-in-law	woman Hitler

Magic Maths

$$1 \times 9 + 2 = 11$$
$$12 \times 9 + 3 = 111$$
$$123 \times 9 + 4 = 1111$$
$$1234 \times 9 + 5 = 11111$$
$$12345 \times 9 + 6 = 111111$$
$$123456 \times 9 + 7 = 1111111$$
$$1234567 \times 9 + 8 = 11111111$$
$$12345678 \times 9 + 9 = 111111111$$
$$123456789 \times 9 + 10 = 1111111111$$

Doctor Dementia

Here's another trick of Doctor Dementia to test
your skills... Can you read this (answer on the next
page):

7H15   M3554G3
53RV35   7O PR0V3
H0W   0UR M1ND5 C4N
D0   4M4Z1NG 7H1NG5!
1MPR3551V3   7H1NG5!
1N   7H3 B3G1NN1NG
17   WA5 H4RD BU7
N0W,   0N 7H15 LIN3
Y0UR   M1ND 1S
R34D1NG 17
4U70M471C4LLY
W17H   0U7 3V3N
7H1NK1NG   4B0U7 17,
B3 PROUD! 0NLY
C3R741N   P30PL3 C4N
R3AD   7H15.

☞   ☞   ☞

Doctor Dementia: answer:

THIS   MESSAGE
SERVES   TO PROVE
HOW   OUR MINDS CAN
DO   AMAZING THINGS!
IMPRESSIVE   THINGS!
IN   THE BEGINNING
IT   WAS HARD BUT
NOW,   ON THIS LINE
YOUR   MIND IS
READING IT
AUTOMATICALLY
WITH   OUT EVEN
THINKING   ABOUT IT,
BE PROUD! ONLY
CERTAIN   PEOPLE CAN
READ   THIS.

☺   ☺   ☺

Did You Know:

France was still executing people by guillotine when 'Star Wars: A New Hope' opened in theatres.

Russia has a larger surface area than Pluto (ninth planet from the sun.)

Weird, but Interesting!

If you can raed this, you have a sgtrane mnid, too. Can you raed this? Olny 55 people out of 100 can.

I cdnuolt blveiee that I cluod aulaclty uesdnatnrd what I was rdanieg. The phaonmneal pweor of the hmuan mnid, aoccdrnig to a rscheearch at Cmabrigde Uinervtisy, it dseno't mtaetr in what oerdr the ltteres in a word are, the olny iproamtnt tihng is that the frsit and last ltteer be in the rghit pclae. The rset can be a taotl mses and you can still raed it whotuit a pboerlm. This is bcuseaethe huamn mnid deos not raed ervey lteter by istlef, but the word as a wlohe. Azanmig huh? Yaeh and I awlyas tghuhot slpeling was ipmorantt!

Weird, but Interesting! Answer:

I couldn't believe that I could actually understand what I was reading. The phenomenal power of the human mind, according to research at Cambridge University, it doesn't matter in what order the letters in a word are, the only important thing is that the first and last letter be in the right place. The rest can be a total mess and you can read it without a problem. This is because the human mind does not read every letter by itself, but the word as a whole. Amazing huh? Yeah and I always thought spelling was important!

Strange English

If lawyers are disbarred and clergymen defrocked, then doesn't it follow that:
- electricians can be delighted,
- musicians denoted,
- cowboys deranged,
- models deposed,
- tree surgeons debarked, and
- dry cleaners depressed?

Attributed to both D. Newmann & G. Carlin

☺   ☺   ☺

Don't do this in public

1. Without anyone watching you (they will think you are goofy) and while sitting at your desk in front of your computer, lift your right foot off the floor and make clockwise circles.
2. Now, while doing this, draw the number '6' in the air with your right hand. Your foot will change direction.

I told you so! And there's nothing you can do about it! You and I both know how stupid it is, but before the day is done you are going to try it again, if you've not already done so.

Maths at Work

What Makes 100%?
What does it mean to give MORE than 100%?

Ever wonder about those people who say they are giving more than 100%? We have all been to those meetings where someone wants you to give over 100%. How about achieving 103%? What makes up 100% in life?

Here is a little mathematical puzzle that might help you answer these questions:

If: A B C D E F G H I J K L M N O P Q R S T U V W X Y Z is represented as:
1 2 3 4 5 6 7 8 9 10 11 12 13 14 15 16 17 18 19 20 21 22 23 24 25 26.

Then: Hard = 8 + 1+ 18 + 4 = 31%
Can you work out the values of:

Work =
Hardwork =
Knowledge =
Attitude =
Politics =
Bullshit =
(answer next page)

☞ ☞ ☞

Maths at Work: answer:

Hardwork = 8+1+18+4+23+15+18+11 = 98%
Knowledge = 11+14+15+23+12+5+4+7+5 = 96%
Attitude = 1+20+20+9+20+21+4+5 = 100%
Politics = 16 + 15 + 12 + 9 + 20 + 9 + 3 + 19 = 103%
Bullshit = 2+21+12+12+19+8+9+20 = 103%

So, one can conclude with mathematical certainty that whilst Hardwork and Knowledge will get you close, and attitude will get you there, it is playing office politics and bullshit that will put you over the top.

More Magic Maths!

1 x 8 + 1 = 9
12 x 8 + 2 = 98
123 x 8 + 3 = 987
1234 x 8 + 4 = 9876
12345 x 8 + 5 = 98765
123456 x 8 + 6 = 987654
1234567 x 8 + 7 = 9876543
12345678 x 8 + 8 = 98765432
123456789 x 8 + 9 = 987654321

Who is the Odd Man Out –
and More Importantly - Why?

Lord Stevenson:
former chairman, HBOS *(Halifax Bank of Scotland)*

Sir Fred Goodwin:
former chief executive, RBS *(Royal Bank of Scotland)*

Andy Hornby:
former chief executive, HBOS

Sir Tom McKillop:
former chairman, RBS

John McFall MP:
former chairman of Treasury Select Committee

Alastair Darling:
former Chancellor of the Exchequer

Gordon Brown:
former Prime Minister / Chancellor of the
Exchequer

Sir Terry Wogan:
former presenter of the UK's Radio 2's Breakfast
Show

(answers on next page)

☞ ☞ ☞

If you are thinking Sir Terry Wogan, then you are right!

But the reason might surprise you:

Sir Terry Wogan is the only one out of this motley crew who actually holds *ANY* formal banking qualification.

Worrying isn't it!

☺   ☺   ☺

Haiku for the 21st Century

In Japan, they have (reportedly) replaced the impersonal and unhelpful computer error messages with Haiku poetry messages. Haiku poetry has strict construction rules. Each poem has only 3 lines and a total of 17 syllables: five syllables in the first line, seven in the second, five in the third.

Your file was big.
It might be very useful.
But now it is gone.

The Web site you seek
Cannot be located, but
Countless more exist.

☞   ☞   ☞

Chaos reigns within.
Reflect, repent, and reboot.
Order shall return.

Program aborting:
Close all that you have worked on.
You ask far too much.

Windows has crashed.
I am the Blue Screen of Death.
No one hears your screams.

Yesterday it worked.
Today it is not working.
Windows is like that.

First snow, then silence.
This thousand dollar screen dies
So beautifully

With searching comes loss
And the presence of absence:
"My Novel" not found.

The Tao that is seen
Is not the true Tao-until
You bring fresh toner.

☞   ☞   ☞

Stay the patient course.
Of little worth is your ire.
The network is down.

A crash reduces
Your expensive computer
To a simple stone.

Three things are certain:
Death, taxes and lost data.
Guess which has occurred.

You step in the stream,
But the water has moved on.
This page is not here.

Out of memory.
We wish to hold the whole sky,
But we never will.

Having been erased,
The document you're seeking
Must now be retyped.

Serious error.
All shortcuts have disappeared.
Screen. Mind. Both are blank.

How Well do you Know the Origins of Common Phrases?

1. Where did the 'rule of thumb' phrase originate?

2. How did the game of golf get its name?

3. How did the phrase 'mind your Ps and Qs' originate?

4. How did the word 'honeymoon' originate?

5. How did the phrase 'goodnight, sleep tight' originate?

6. How did the phrase 'Wet your whistle' come from?

And do you know:

7. Who was the first couple to be shown in bed together (on prime time TV in the Uunited States)?

8. Who can read smaller print: men or women?

9. Who can hear better: men or women?

10. What colour was Coca Cola originally?

☞ ☞ ☞

11. Which American state has the highest percentage of people that walk to work?

12. What percentage of Africa is wilderness?

13. What percentage of North America is wilderness?

14. What was the first novel written on a typewriter?

15. What is the only mobile national monument in the USA?

16. Which historic kings/world leaders are represented on a normal pack of playing cards?

17. If you were to spell out the numbers (one, two, three etc) how far would you get before writing the letter "a"?

18. What do bulletproof vests, fire escapes, windshield wipers, and laser printers all have in common?

☞ ☞ ☞

Origins of common phrases: answers

1. In the 1400's a law was set forth in England
    that a man was allowed to beat his wife with a
    stick no thicker than his thumb. Hence we
    have 'the rule of thumb'.

2. Many years ago in Scotland, a new game was
    invented. It was ruled: 'Gentlemen Only ...
    Ladies Forbidden' = GOLF.

3. In English pubs, ale is ordered by pints and
    quarts... So in old England, when customers
    got unruly, the bartender would yell at them
    "Mind your pints and quarts, and settle
    down."

4. It was the accepted practice in Babylon 4,000
    years ago that for a month after a wedding,
    the bride's father would supply his son in law
    with all the mead he could drink. Mead is a
    honey beer and because their calendar was
    lunar based, this period was called the honey
    month, which we know today as the
    honeymoon.

☞ ☞ ☞

5. In Shakespeare's time, mattresses were secured on bed frames by ropes. When you pulled on the ropes the mattress tightened, making the bed firmer to sleep on. Hence the phrase 'goodnight, sleep tight.'

6. Many years ago in England, pub frequenters had a whistle baked into the rim, or handle, of their ceramic cups. When they needed a refill, they used the whistle to get some service. 'Wet your whistle' is the phrase inspired by this practice.

7. The first couple to be shown in bed together on prime time TV were Fred and Wilma Flintstone.

8. Men can read smaller print than women can.

9. Women can hear better than men.

10. Coca Cola was originally green!

11. The state with the highest percentage of people who walk to work: Alaska

12. 28% of Africa is wilderness.

13. 38% of North America is wilderness.

14. The first novel ever written on a typewriter was Tom Sawyer.

15. The San Francisco cable cars are the only mobile National Monument.

16. The kings/historic leaders represented in a deck of playing cards are:
King David (spades),
Charlemagne (hearts),
Alexander, the Great (clubs),
Julius Caesar (diamonds)

17. The first time the letter "a" occurs is one thousand!

18. Bulletproof vests, fire escapes, windshield wipers, and laser printers were all invented by women.

☺   ☺   ☺

And more Magic Maths

$$1 \times 1 = 1$$
$$11 \times 11 = 121$$
$$111 \times 111 = 12321$$
$$1111 \times 1111 = 1234321$$
$$11111 \times 11111 = 123454321$$

Try 111111x111111, 1111111x1111111 etc

Did you know that:

If a statue in the park of a person on a horse has both front legs in the air, the person died in battle. If the horse has one front leg in the air the person died as a result of wounds received in battle. If the horse has all four legs on the ground, the person died of natural causes.

111,111,111 x 111,111,111 =
12,345,678,987,654,321

You can't lick your elbow!

And finally at least 75% of people who read that last fact will try to lick their elbow!

☺   ☺   ☺

We hope you have enjoyed reading this book as much as we enjoyed collating it for you.

Thank you for supporting our charities.

Tim & Rick Stapenhurst.

And remember:
If at first you don't succeed, sky diving is not for you!

Index of Jokes

A Request

This book has been donated by the authors on the understanding that ALL proceeds from the sale of this book go to the charity to which they donated the book.

Where this book has been bought through Amazon the authors will donate all royalties to charity.

When you have finished with this book, please pass it to a friend, return it to the author (to donate to another charity) or dispose of it in the paper recycling. Please do not donate it to another charity.

We respectfully ask book re-sellers not to offer this book for sale without first contacting the authors.

Thank you.

For queries and further information contact info@stapenhurstpublications.com

Made in the USA
Columbia, SC
23 December 2017